A Naturalist at Large

A Naturalist at Large

The Best Essays of Bernd Heinrich

———◦◦◦◇◇◦◦◦———

BERND HEINRICH

Houghton Mifflin Harcourt

Boston   New York

2018

For information about permission to reproduce selections from this book, write
to trade.permissions@hmhco.com or to Permissions, Houghton Mifflin Harcourt
Publishing Company, 3 Park Avenue, 19th Floor, New York, New York 10016.

hmhco.com

Library of Congress Cataloging-in-Publication Data is available.
ISBN 978-0-544-98683-1

Printed in the United States of America
DOC 10 9 8 7 6 5 4 3 2 1

The following essays have appeared elsewhere in slightly different form:
Natural History: "Life in the Soil," "Rock-Solid Foundation," "The Spreading
Chestnut Tree," "When the Bough Bends," "O Tannenbaum," "Reading Tree
Leaves," "Hot- and Cold-Blooded Moths" (under the title "False Assumptions:
A Matter of Degrees"), "Woolly and Wondrous," "Winter Guests," "Arctic
Bumblebees" (under the title "The Antifreeze of Bees"), "Beating the Heat, and
Killing with Heat," "Beetles and Blooms" (under the title "Bedouins, Blooms, and
Beetles"), "Cooperative Undertaking: Teaming with Mites," "Whirligig Beetles:
Quick Paddlers," "A Birdbrain Nevermore," "Phoebe Diary," "Conversation with
a Sapsucker," "Kinglets' Realm of Cold," "The Diabolical Nightjar," "Hidden
Sweets," "Cohabiting with Elephants: A Browsing Relationship," "The Hunt:
A Matter of Perspective," "Synchronicity: Amplifying the Signal," "Curious
Yellow: A Foray into Iris Behavior," "Twists and Turns," "Birds, Bees, and Beauty:
Adaptive Aesthetics." *Audubon:* "Ravens on my Mind," "Birds Coloring Their
Eggs" (under the title "Why Is a Robin's Egg Blue?"). *Orion:* "Ravens and the
Inaccessible." *Outside:* "Hawk Watching," "Endurance Predator." *New York Times:*
"Hibernation, Insulation, and Caffeination," "What Bees and Flowers Know."
Field Notes: "Seeing the Light in the Forest."

*I dedicate this book to Professor James R. Cook,
my academic adviser at the University of Maine,
research associate, and dear friend, who inspired me
and steered me onto the path to science*

Contents

CONTENTS

Introduction

NATURAL HISTORIANS MAKE OBSERVATIONS THAT PROMPT questions, whose answers lead to an understanding of life in its various dimensions. In this collection of natural history essays, I hope to provide a general audience with examples of the links between such observations and the science of biology. My chosen topics are derived from common observations of nature. I wanted to highlight some of the stories that I have found most exciting through the years and had published in *Natural History* magazine and other venues. Some are the result of decades-long studies, while others were instigated by anecdotes that inspired shorter periods of curiosity. In winnowing through essays to include in this volume, I exercised a bias in selecting a variety of subjects that depict the interconnectedness of all of life, and their relation to our individual human lives.

It seems to me that the process of understanding nature at large has become increasingly difficult. To study it in depth and scientifically may require specialization, which can at the same time remove us from the world we experience, making investigations and conclusions abstract. My hope, however, is that these essays will stimulate and encourage participation and the desire to experience nature not only through science but also through direct contact.

I am fortunate to have had unique opportunities for extensive and intimate contact with the natural world as well as scientific grounding. This combination was made possible by the enthusiastic predecessors who provided me with experience and inspiration: rich soil to grow on.

My father, Gerd, made me go out with him to hunt ichneumon wasps and trap mice, and at age six gave me instructions on how to properly pin beetles for a scientific collection. My mother, Hildegarde, taught me how to skin and stuff small birds and mammals for museum specimens, and how to dry and preserve plants. Rolf Grantsau showed me how to make and use a slingshot and introduced me to a paintbrush. Floyd Adams told me about the woodpecker (the flicker) that feeds on the ground and the songbird that flies like a quail (the meadowlark). His wife, Leona, was upset when I shot a hummingbird with my slingshot in her blueberry patch in bloom in the yard. Floyd took me along with his kids to go bee-lining, raccoon hunting, and white perch fishing at night on Pease Pond. Phil Potter taught me how to use a .30-30 Winchester rifle and how to handle a canoe, fly rod, ax, pitchfork, and hoe. I thank Dick Cook for giving me confidence and joy in doing meaningful experiments suitable for publication in technical journals. George Bartholomew helped me consider every word in writing up scientific results. I remember all these people fondly and appreciate them still, for they all live on in spirit, having helped create the work presented here.

I thank my agent, Sandy Dijkstra, whose upbeat nudging instigated and then encouraged me to write another book in the first place. My editor, Deanne Urmy of Houghton Mifflin Harcourt, was always figuratively looking over my shoulder to see the larger picture, and I appreciate Susanna Brougham's careful eye in spotting the inconsistencies, though all errors that remain are strictly my own. Lisa Glover graciously coordinated this book's production. Lastly and mostly, I'm grateful to Lynn Jennings for her patience during my prolonged time spent at the writing desk, her deciphering of my script and typing, and her active support as a sounding board for ideas. The Maine woods have not been the same since she arrived, and they never will be. Craig Neff and Pamelia Markwood, of the Naturalist's Notebook of Seal Harbor, Maine, archived my illustrations so that I could make them available here.

Think you that the rounded rock marked with parallel scratches calls up as much poetry in an ignorant mind as in the mind of a geologist, who knows that over this rock a glacier slid a million years ago? The truth is, that those who have never entered upon scientific pursuits know not a tithe of the poetry by which they are surrounded — whoever has not in youth collected plants and insects, knows not half the halo of interest which lanes and hedgerows can assume.

— Herbert Spencer, English biologist, 1820–1903

FROM THE EARTH UP

Life in the Soil

Natural History, November 2014

PAPA, MAMUSHA, MY SISTER MARIANNE, AND I WERE FOR six years quartered in a one-room hut in a dark forest in northern Germany right after World War II. Towering pines, spruce, and beech shaded the ground except for a small sloping patch in front of the cabin. Light snow had recently covered the ground, and now, after a warm spring rain, it had become black, and that made me notice something marvelous by our doorstep. From one day to the next, I saw a small patch on the dirt turning a luminous green. Perhaps the next day or so after that, the patch had expanded over the black ground: I was mesmerized by this verdant, magically spreading circle of grass blades.

This was, as far as I can remember, my earliest moment of wonder. Had grass been underfoot before, I would have hardly noticed it, from seeing it all the time. But watching that single patch expand from one day to the next was a moment of magic and mystery, maybe even of ecstasy, forever stamped into my memory.

Even so, for a long time the dirt the grass had spawned from remained for me merely something crumbly under the soles of my feet and between my toes. It was the sand on a mile or so of the wooded road between our hut and the village school. Shiny green beetles flashed in front of me on my walks, and after a brief zigzag-ging flight, where they glinted like jewels in the sun, they landed a few yards ahead. We called them "sand beetles," and later I knew them as tiger beetles. Although I couldn't fly, I could run, and it felt good to be on par with such gorgeous company.

Tiger beetles (of the family Cicindelidae) are related to cara-bids, which are commonly called ground beetles, or *Laufkäfer*. Ground beetles do not fly, but they all run (which is reflected in their German name, derived from *laufen*, "to run"). These earth-bound beetles soon became my passion, to have and to hold. It came through the influence of my father, a biologist. In order to get some cash he was now digging tree stumps out of the ground that had been left by the occupying British soldiers who had har-vested the trees. He earned a few pfennigs selling the wood. But he decided the pits he was digging might be adapted to serve as traps to catch mice and shrews. It was exciting for me to accom-pany him, ever more so because ground beetles fell into the pits too, and he showed me how to preserve and thus to collect them like some other kids then collected stamps. He gave me a field guide to identify those that I had and those I might someday find. I soon knew them by name: the giant black *Carabus coriaceus*, the dark-bluish *C. intricatus*, the shiny copper *C. cancellatus* (and its look-alike, *C. concolor*), and the deep-green *C. auratus*. The merit of those intricately sculpted beetles was not simply that they were beautiful, but also that I could find them merely by scan-ning the ground wherever I walked. Even more merrily, I could catch them.

I thought of these, my old carabids, with a start, with a nostalgic recognition, when recently — now in Maine, on a new continent — I dug out the pit for our privy. There, several feet down in the dirt, I unearthed a *Carabus*. It was metallic black, sculpted in lines and pits, and its edges glistened deep purple. Not having collected these beetles for a long time, I did not know the name of this species nor what it was doing underground, but I captured it in a photograph. Perhaps as a larva it had burrowed in that spot and metamorphosed to become an adult, or maybe it had hibernated there in the winter, or was attempting to escape heat or drought. But in any case, it had likely fed on snails, and the snails on grass. It was of the soil, which I was preparing to receive my wastes. And

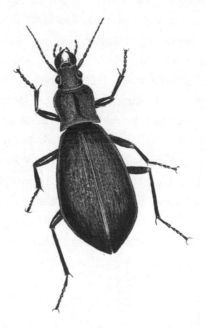

Carabus intricatus, *a species I had in my childhood collection.*

this same receptive soil would also receive all of me, eventually, to convert me to grass, trees, flowers, and more. For the time being, though, an American chestnut tree I had planted years earlier, as well as nearby sugar maples, would grow well because of their proximity to the privy.

I used the dirt from the pit excavation to make a raised garden bed in which I planted potatoes. I stuck several of them into this dirt, and presto, come fall — it seemed too good to be true — there were perfect and delicious Yukon Golds. My partner, Lynn, saw the magic, and before I knew it we had an even bigger bed of potatoes, beans climbing a pole, snap peas growing on a chicken-wire fence, and little green sprouts of kale, carrots, and lettuce. We watched with eager participation as the emerging green dots in the dark dirt first turned into shoots, and we would harvest potatoes in August for eating in winter.

There is more to be had from dirt than food. I think Thoreau knew this well and maybe said it better 175 years ago. Old Henry (if he'd excuse me for being familiar) was "determined to know beans," and having made himself a two-and-a-half-acre bean field, he tended and hoed it daily from "five o'clock in the morning till noon." He came to "love" and "cherish" his beans and wrote, "they attached me to the earth, and so I got strength like Antaeus." Working alone and with his hands, he became, as he said, "much more intimate with my beans than usual." Along the way he concluded that "labor of the hands, even when pursued to the verge of drudgery, is perhaps never the worst form of idleness." And he told the reasons why.

When tending his bean field, Thoreau was "attracted by the passage of wild pigeons"; he sometimes "watched a pair of hen-hawks circling high in the sky," heard the brown thrasher sing, and with his hoe "turned up a sluggish portentous and outlandish spotted salamander." His enterprise was "not that I wanted beans to eat," nor was it likely for "leaving a pecuniary profit."

I'm in rapport with his romantic ideal and with his statement that when he "paused to lean on my hoe, these sounds and sights I heard and saw anywhere in the row became part of the inexhaustible entertainment which the country offers" — as opposed, I suppose, to those summer days "which some of my contemporaries devoted to the fine arts in Boston and Rome" as entertainment, instead. Perhaps this vibrant "idleness" is what Thoreau cherished most.

Most would, however, want to "get real" when it comes to dirt and work. We do not generally hoe beans in order to hear the brown thrasher, or to exhume a spotted salamander as an end in itself. Thoreau gets real by giving an exact economic enumeration of his work. He itemizes monetary costs and profits, in which overall bean-patch costs added up in his accounting to $14.72 and 1/2 cent, with a profit of $8.71 and 1/2 cent.

To our minds now, old Henry pretty much worked that summer in his two-and-a-half-acre bean patch for nothing. The garden patch that Lynn and I worked on sporadically our first summer, making a garden from what was before only a brushy rock-filled field, allows for some comparisons. We saw no passenger pigeons but we got pleasures from our garden similar to what Henry got from his. Plus, we enjoy companionship, which old Henry did not appear to pursue. So for us it was a win-win situation with the dirt, in more ways than two. But I also suspect our dirt will before the start of winter become a winning economic proposition as well. And so was Henry's, despite what he may have implied, and we inferred.

Our dirt patch is sixteen hundred square feet (0.037 acres); his was about 70 times larger. He spent $3.12 on seed, and we spent $94. Thus, overall, in terms of our money, he paid about 30 times less overall, but on a per-acre basis, in dollar amount, he paid 2,100 times less. Take outside labor: his "ploughing/harrowing/farrowing" cost him $7.50. (This amount irked him, because in *Walden*, he added a comment — "Too much" — for emphasis next to it.) How much is his "Too much"? Lynn and I paid our neighbor, Mike Pratt, $150 to harrow our plot (from brush and rock-cobbled soil), which, as already mentioned, is 70 times smaller than Henry's. But Henry did not pay 70 times more. Instead, he paid 20 times less overall, which comes to 1,400 times less per unit acre than we paid. Similarly, our total pecuniary costs were 1,960 times more than his, prorated per acre. My point: inflation since the time of Thoreau's bean patch (of 175 years ago) has reduced the worth of a dollar about 2,000 times from what it used to be. Thus, Thoreau's seemingly trivial profit of $8.71 and a half cent is actually a hefty $17,430, in terms of the dollar now. (His seeming pettiness, accounting to the last half cent, is thus more like figuring to within ten dollars now.)

How many young people today could earn $17,000 in a summer by working forenoons in a bean field, and having the rest of the day off for "other affairs"? None! But it was not the amount of money Thoreau made from his bean field that he rhapsodized about. It was the ancillary "profit." Now we are hard put to get a fraction of the pecuniary profit he earned, and if we do it is usually at the cost of the other satisfactions that a country life close to the dirt provides, and that we now all too commonly lack. Thoreau derided husbandry as he saw it then as pursued with "irreverent haste and heedlessness . . . [with] our object being to have large farms and large crops merely." His conclusion that "I will not plant beans and corn with so much industry another summer" suggests he felt that even his "industry" was already too much.

Turn now to the other Henry, a Maine writer a century later, near the arguable beginning of industrial agriculture. In his book *Northern Farm*, Henry Beston reminds us that "the shadow of any man is but for a time cast upon the grass of any field. What remains is the earth, the mother of life." And he concludes, "When farming becomes purely utilitarian, something perishes . . . sometimes it is the human beings who practice this economy, and oftenest of all it is a destruction of both land and man."

As a fellow human — united with the two earlier Henrys not by artificial or perceived boundaries but by our universal bonds to the soil, the link that connects all of Life — I grow beans for more than utilitarian purposes. Our farming may be token, but like the blades of grass that first sparked my interest in living things, the activity is a visceral and sometimes an ecstatic reminder of the context of our relationship to the earth and other organisms.

Rock-Solid Foundation

Natural History, February 2017

OF ALL THE GORGEOUS OLD TREES I'VE SEEN OVER THE years, none has stood out more than the massive, ancient yellow birch, *Betula alleghaniensis*, that is about a mile from our cabin here in the Maine woods. Although I've seen it for at least thirty years, I had never tried to know it. I had never thought about why this tree, or yellow birches in general, might be special until I reflected recently on the fact that they can sprout on rocks. Lichen and moss — both of which dry out for months and then rehydrate — grow on rocks, but trees need access to constant moisture. How can yellow birches take root and live where other tree species don't?

This yellow birch is the oldest tree in these woods. How did it manage to survive so long? It flowers regularly and has likely produced seeds for at least two centuries. Around it lie the rotting trunks of other kinds of trees, none as old, yet no new yellow birch recruits have sprung up near this tree. Instead, it is surrounded by spruce, fir, and maples, red and sugar, which have filled in what was once a sheep pasture, cleared by settlers in the late eighteenth century from an old-growth forest. It's a wonder that the settlers left this lone tree standing.

Yellow birch trees are best known for their smooth bark with a gorgeous golden sheen. This tree, which I mentally claim as mine, sheds its bark in large brittle flakes. Its core has rotted away so its exact age is hard to determine. Extrapolations from the minuscule growth rings of its outer shell would greatly overestimate its age. My conservative estimate is that it has logged three centuries. At a height of forty-five feet, it is dwarfed by the 150-year-old white pines upslope from it and by the 200-year-old sugar maples that run along an old fence line. But in girth, at a circumference of eleven feet, it exceeds all other trees in this forest. It rises from the ground like a huge shaggy chimney. At the top, it has an opening into its hollow core, reminiscent of the seventy-foot rotting syca-more that John James Audubon found near Louisville, Kentucky, in 1808. It was home to an estimated nine thousand chimney swifts whose roaring noise in the hollow tree amazed him. Swifts may have lived in this one too, seventy years ago, when they were common in this area; several pair used to nest in the chimney of the nearby farmstead where we once lived. My tree's large inner chamber is also accessible to mammals; two feet aboveground there is a hole large enough for fishers, porcupines, or a small bear.

On numerous occasions I've peppered the ground with seeds of various tree species to watch the battle of seedlings on the unal-tered forest floor. Nothing ever sprouted from the thousands of birch seeds I spread. On the other hand, a yellow birch tree that I planted near our cabin took off, and is rising two feet in height per year.

Lack of yellow birch seedlings is not from a lack of seeds.

Wanting numbers, I counted, on average, 130 seeds per conelike fruit. Multiplying that figure by the number of cones per twig and the number of twigs of an average-sized tree, I estimate that an average-sized, mature yellow birch produces an annual crop of 19.5 million seeds. Unlike beechnut seeds carried by birds or poplar seeds scattered by the wind, yellow birch seeds don't spread far from their source. It seems these seeds need to be spectacularly lucky to find precisely the right spot, or conditions, to sprout.

In another part of the forest, I found a nearly straight swath of yellow birch seedlings — all near the same age — which had sprung up along an old, heavily used logging path by a large seed-bearing yellow birch tree. Apparently, the young trees were able to take root because the soil had been exposed. This hypothesis was supported by another logging area where the ground had been badly scarred by heavy machinery. Young yellow birches were sprouting in the areas disturbed by the machinery. The age of the seedlings coincided with the time when the logging had stopped.

I became increasingly interested in where yellow birches *might* grow, because there were many tall and healthy yellow birch trees throughout the woods that stood on rocks. Yet near these seeding trees, I found no seedlings, despite the open spaces on the forest floor. However, I did find young yellow birches, along with young balsam firs and spruces, growing on tree stumps. This was a clue.

Conifers occasionally grew on rotting stumps but not on rocks. All the yellow birches I saw — unlike the firs and spruces — spread one or several roots over the edge of their seedling perches on rocks or stumps and sank them into the ground. Since no seedlings of any kind were growing surrounding the same rocks or stumps, I suspected that the layer of shed leaves on the ground could be excluding yellow birch trees from taking root. But how could shed leaves, the potential mulch of maples, ash, beech, and oaks, be excluding the sprouting of yellow birch seedlings? One hypothesis for lack of seedlings under a tree is growth inhibitors, called allelochemicals. However, in this case, as I will show, ecological and evolutionary perspectives suggest more likely possibilities. It begins with seed size, and soil.

Although speck-sized yellow birch seeds are more abundant than seeds from competing species, they carry little parental investment of food in the form of fat, carbohydrate, or protein, to get seedlings started. They need such resources immediately upon sprouting. Forest clearings, such as those from logging operations, open the canopy to sunlight and provide an opportunity for new growth, because the light is available to all trees and other plants that have seeds or saplings in place. At first, all are on an equal footing. Then the race begins. Acorn, chestnut, and beechnut seeds have huge energy reserves. They have the ability to start growing wherever they are, even when buried under a thick layer of fallen leaves. Birch seeds, however, lacking such reserves, instead have a mechanism that gives them a chance, in open areas, to quickly reach water in moist soil for sprouting, and to use the light from above for growing: stumps, rocks with damp moss, or patches of bare earth provide a perch, and fast root growth access to water below the perch. A yellow birch seedling's odds of surviving are still low in comparison to those of trees that provide parental investment of food resources. Yet when both reach similar size, their growth strategies converge. They all fight for the light. The yellow birch, however, has an added twist.

Not only do trees grow straight up to reach the most available light — they also spread laterally to reach light from the sides. In a forest, as hundreds of seedlings per square foot begin to grow, each gets a diminishing share of sunlight from above and laterally. Within several years after an opening in a canopy, thickets result, and soon not a single new seedling is produced. Within a coni-fer stand, there is almost permanent dark shade. Not even moss or lichen can grow. In deciduous woods with big broadleaf trees, the seasonal leaf fall creates temporary light in the beginning of spring. Lichen and moss have a chance to take hold atop exposed rocks, stumps, and logs. However, seeds that fall in the deep layer of shed leaves are doomed unless they are laden with enough en-ergy reserves to punch through to sunlight.

Conversely, envision a tiny birch seed landing in moss on a rock that is sticking up above the leaves. The spongelike moss periodi-cally holds enough moisture for the seed to sprout. If the two tiny green leaves of the sprig can capture enough energy from the sun — when it is high in the sky in spring and fall — and ambient car-bon dioxide in combination with moisture from the moss, then the seedling's root system can begin to grow and probe, reaching out from its rock perch. The faster and longer it can grow, the greater the chance it has of reaching the ground, and water. Once a root reaches moisture, it responds quickly by enlarging and taking on ever more water and resources for growth.

In trying to answer what adaptation might allow yellow birch to grow on rocks where no other trees grow, I speculated that the species depends on the rapid growth rate of its roots. I examined a decaying pine log in a deciduous forest that was located near a large yellow birch tree. The forest floor was covered by a deep layer of leaves. As expected, there were no yellow birch seedlings grow-ing on this leaf-covered ground, but a moss-covered log hosted fourteen of them. They ranged in height from a few inches to sev-eral feet. I pulled on the root of one of the larger trees and man-aged to extract six feet of it. Along that length, the root tapered from 2.1 to 1.5 millimeters in diameter. I calculated that if the rate of diameter reduction from trunk to root tip was uniform for the whole root, and the tip diameter was 0.3 millimeters, then the root would be about twenty-five feet long. The root looked and felt like rope. I could not break it by tensile pulling. The root's side branches tapered in size to thin threads and continued on to what looked more like spiderweb silk, with innumerable side branches that resembled sprouting hairs. Next I pulled up a three-year-old yellow birch seedling, roots and all. It had a main trunk of twenty-three inches, with three side twigs of three-, five-, and eight-inch lengths. I was again unable to pull the roots all the way out to their tips. However, I did manage to follow them for twelve, twenty, twenty-four, and twenty-nine inches, respectively. Given the larger side branches from these that I had managed to follow, this tree had at least four and a half times more root length than stem-limb length. The roots were sufficient in length to reach the ground, several times over, from the top of the log where the seedling perched. Extreme thinness would presumably allow fast growth. The seedling would need a relatively short period of dampness and light to create its pipeline to water and other nutrients.

The rush to reach soil, with its water and nutrients, is only the third step in the tree's strategy — after seed dispersal to a suitable place and germination. The next struggle is mainly for light, to secure the energy from sunshine to fix carbon dioxide. Upward growth may be the best all-around strategy — a race to the top as neighbors crowd in from all sides. But the lateral option is not without merit. When I started sketching tree shapes, it became obvious that there are compromises between growing upward and outward. Both options are executed to different degrees. In thickets where a mix of deciduous trees battled — red oaks, American ash, red and sugar maples — all shoots went straight up. Branching to the sides was minimal. As branches become shaded from the tree's own leaves from above — and from the sides — they die and shed; resources are continually allocated to the top.

The same process occurs with all densely crowded trees, but beech and yellow birch trees hold on to their lower branches longer before shedding them. As a result, the lower branches of young trees of those species grow horizontally until a later age. Apparently, they are more shade-tolerant; filtered light under a canopy is sufficient to keep those limbs growing. Thus, as other trees become long, thin poles, holding up an often very small crown, yellow birch and beech become shaped more like conifers (that is, triangular, with tiers of branches that spread laterally). With the yellow birch, however, that shaping changes radically when it reaches an opening in the canopy. The tree then produces a giant crown that spreads in all directions. Only at that point does the birch shed its lower branches and thicken its trunk. Having gained this knowledge, and with my sketches of young and old yellow birch trees in hand, I went back to my Methuselah birch to try to reconstruct its history of growth.

The first striking feature of the tree was its tall, straight trunk. If it had started life in an open area, then its lower branches would have reached out to the sides and kept on growing. The tree might have ended up with several trunks, growing in different directions. However, this tree displayed thick branches only at a height of thirty feet and above. There were no large exposed rocks on the gentle slope where the tree grew, and it is too old to have started on soil disturbed by human activity, such as logging or farming. But a burn could have provided open space. In such a case, layers of fallen leaves would not have excluded a yellow birch seedling: it would have been on the open ground and under the open sky. So, it likely grew up along with fir and spruce seedlings in a thicket like those that start after burns. The tree would have pruned off its lower limbs as it grew with its rivals, because post-burn conifer thickets are so dark that even a yellow birch would have to join the race to the top. But firs are short-lived, and the long-lived yellow birch would have ultimately been left to spread its limbs. It would have grown taller and wider. For a century or two, it likely stood high in hurricanes and ice storms. The storms may have pruned off its top and its biggest branches, so the tree gradually assumed its present shape.

Porcupines did their part as well. They routinely debark beech and birch trees, gnawing off huge patches of bark at ground level. This behavior usually kills a tree unless a strip of live bark is left. The wood under the debarking, however, is always killed, and in a usually damp northern forest, rot hollows out trees. Fresh wood grows in from the sides of the wound. The hole and the hollow of this tree may have resulted from such an encounter, which could have happened two or three hundred years ago. Rot then weakened the tree's top, making it vulnerable to damage by weather.

This Methuselah still has crown enough to compete with the new growth of maples, firs, spruce, and red oaks growing under it. It still has enough top to reach direct sunlight. When I last checked, some of its top branches, like those of all other yellow birches of embryo-bearing age, were loaded with seed cones. I estimated 500 fruits (about 65,000 seeds). The goldfinches will stay the winter to feed on them in crowds. The ruffed grouse rely heavily on the birch's buds in winter. In early spring, the buds burst to reveal the tree's pale-green leaves, along with its tasseled flowers. Every seed a tree produces over its long life could theoretically become another tree, but it pays to keep in mind observed reality — on average, only one will make it to adulthood.

The Spreading Chestnut Tree

Natural History, April 2016

IMAGINE A TREE OVER 10 FEET THICK, TOWERING MORE than 120 feet high, with light, cream-colored flowers that made mountains appear to be covered in snow. The American chestnut (*Castanea dentata*) once had the majesty and presence to transform landscapes when it was in bloom. It was the king of eastern forests, accounting for an estimated one-quarter of the woodland that ran from southern Maine to Georgia. It was a climax species, meaning a species that remains unchanged in a stable environment, and of critical importance for wildlife and humans. Its leathery-skinned nuts fed multitudes, including deer, turkey, passenger pigeons, blue jays, squirrels, and people. The nuts were a delicious mainstay for many settlers. People used the chestnut's bark for tanning hides. Its smooth-grained lightweight wood was as easy to work, and it was highly rot-resistant. As a construction material, it was superior for fence posts, barn and house timbers, railroad ties, furniture, cradles, and coffins. It was known as the cradle-to-grave tree.

In 1904, however, an unimaginable disaster struck. Hermann Merkel, the chief forester at the New York Zoological Park (now the Bronx Zoo), noticed that a few of the chestnut trees that lined the park's walkways were diseased. A year later, all of the chestnut trees in the park were infected. The blight was caused by a fungus (*Diaporthe parasitica*), apparently transported to the United States on fungus-resistant Asian chestnut trees that had been imported to a nursery in Flushing, New York, in 1876. From its first detection in 1904, the blight spread at a rate of twenty to fifty miles per year, seemingly killing every tree in its wake, an estimated 3.5 to 4 billion. The infestation occurred at a time when the American chestnut appeared to be expanding west to Indiana and Illinois. By the 1930s, the reign of the American chestnut was over. Most of the trees were gone, although some aging survivors persisted in Michigan.

In the 1970s, the retiree James Raymond Comp of Cadillac, Michigan, began, at age seventy-three, to map the chestnut trees that he knew still existed in his area. Many of them were eighty to a hundred years old and had been planted by pioneers from New York and Pennsylvania. Comp located more than a thousand American chestnut trees around Cadillac alone, with many still bearing fruit. He became obsessed with these trees in Michigan that for some reason were resistant to the fungal blight. Comp was convinced that propagating the offspring of these trees might rescue the species. The U.S. Forest Service rebuffed his suggestion that the agency become involved because, by that time, it appeared to be an established fact that the fungus was 100 percent lethal.

Undaunted, Comp appealed to the Wexford Soil Conservation District to join his mission. This county organization had a history, dating back to 1945, of working on conservation projects with farmers and other citizens. Comp was able to convince the conservation district of Wexford and that of its neighboring county, Missaukee, to spread Michigan chestnut seeds. In fact, the Forest Service's view regarding the fungus was overly categorical: the blight, which had expanded rapidly in eastern forests, had slowed dramatically by the time it reached Michigan. Either the fungus or the trees had changed. Some trees at the western end of the range, which had been infected in the 1940s and should have died within four years, were still alive thirty years later. Their cankers from the infection had healed. A possible explanation for the slowdown came from Europe. The European chestnut (*Castanea sativa*) had also been devastated by the blight, but in 1976 researchers discovered that a virus (in the Hypoviridae family) had attacked the fungus and greatly reduced its impact, thereby enabling European chestnuts to survive.

After this discovery, it was hypothesized that this virus was also present in Michigan and accounted for the state's blight-resistant trees. The mapping program started by Comp was joined by Lawrence Brewer, a student at Hope College in Holland, Michigan, who located more than ten thousand surviving trees. At that point, Michigan seemed to be the only U.S. state where significant numbers of chestnuts survived. (Since then, groves of hundreds to thousands of healthy American chestnut trees have been discovered near West Salem, Wisconsin, and Warm Springs, Georgia, and individual specimens exist in other states, including Maine.) The efforts of one determined individual joined by his friends and local organizations eventually led to the establishment of the American Chestnut Council. Based in Cadillac, Michigan, the council collects seeds from Michigan's blight-resistant trees and works with nurseries that grow seedlings for sale to the public.

I had already joined Comp's quest when I bought twenty-five of the Michigan seedlings and planted them near my cabin in Maine in 1982. I did not expect to live long enough to see them flower, much less to produce seeds, because even if they should survive, there were no trees nearby to pollinate them. Nevertheless, it was a thrill to see some of my seedlings take root, shoot up, and expand their toothed leaves, which look like oversized beech leaves (the American chestnut being in the Fagaceae, or beech tree, family).

Beyond my expectations, I did see my trees flower years later.

A variety of beetles, moths, flies, bees, and wasps were attracted to the musty-smelling, long white tassel-like inflorescences. Small green fruits formed from the female flowers, and they grew into nearly baseball-sized green spiny fruits — called burrs — which typically pack three leathery nuts each. However, all the fruits that I eagerly examined at their first appearance lacked fertile nuts. As anticipated, the flowers producing these fruits had not been pollinated.

The trees continued to grow at a rate of about two feet per year, and when they were well over a foot thick at chest height, they still showed no sign of disease. A visiting member of the Maine branch of the American Chestnut Foundation pronounced them to be pure American chestnuts. Having four healthy American chestnuts on my property, grown well beyond the juvenile stage, was more than I had hoped for. Soon there were more.

One day in late October, after most of the forest tree leaves had fallen, I found a clump of three small tree saplings whose leaves had the typical chestnut tree saw-tooth edges. After scraping away some soil, I saw the year-old shells of American chestnuts from which the seedlings had sprung. Baby chestnuts were growing in the woods near my cabin! There must have been cross-pollination among the four surviving trees after all. Finding these seedlings, and later more, raised questions worth exploring.

The burrs that I had first picked up from the ground under the

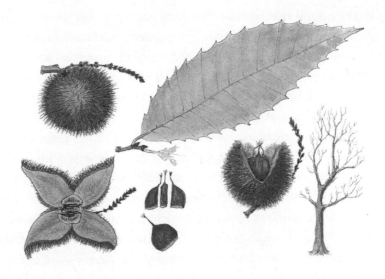

Leaf, fruit, and seeds of the native American chestnut tree.

trees were shed early because they were not pollinated and were therefore not developing seeds; the trees had shed an unprofitable investment of energy. The fruit from pollinated flowers with viable seeds, on the other hand, had continued to stay on the tree until ripe. Their distribution far into the woods was intriguing. Near the parent trees, planted at the edge of my clearing, I found no seedlings. Who or what had dispersed the chestnuts? Every fall thereafter, I watched for potential nut spreaders.

One fall, I noticed a flock of blue jays descend on the chestnut trees and, for about a week, pick nuts out of the spiky fruit. The jays had timed their foraging to coincide with the moment when the four exterior flanges of the burrs had curled outward to expose soft, silky interiors. No jays opened still-closed burrs. They would pack two or three nuts into their throat pouch and then fly off over the forest, presumably to cache them on or in the ground. It is well known that corvid birds scatter-hoard, taking each load to a different place. The 238 baby chestnuts that I have located over time have indeed been widely distributed. To no surprise, many have sprung up in groups of two and three, but some have been in clumps of up to ten seedlings, and one clump contained twenty. The large clumps that I first found were surprising because the jays usually carried no more than three nuts at a time, and they are not known to cache successive loads at the same spot. Identifying the distributor of these chestnut seedlings, I figured, could prove relevant to the revival of the chestnut.

Several gray squirrels visited the chestnut trees that same fall, but they stayed in the crowns and fed on the fruit. Red squirrels arrived before the nuts were ripe, when the burrs were tightly closed. I heard a series of thumps as tennis-ball-sized burrs hit the ground. The squirrels were snipping them off at the stem. The squirrels then descended the trees, picked up the burrs, chewed them open, and ate the nuts on the spot. Given the burrs' thick protective shell and their spines, which make them look like sea urchins, the process was slow and potentially painful. During that time, I did not see any squirrels run off with a burr or a seed.

The following autumn was different. There had been a good crop of beechnuts and the jays seemed to ignore the chestnuts. When the burrs opened, however, a red squirrel was in the tree and, this year, it did not snip off burrs. Again and again it ran up the tree, came down with a nut, and ran off into the woods, each time using a similar route. I surmised it was caching nuts. There was a premium for doing so because thousands of nuts were suddenly and easily available without the thick barrier of spines.

The squirrel seemed to be taking the nuts to the same area, if not to the same particular place. I waited until the squirrel made another run to the top of the tree, then I ran into the woods from where it had just come. I hid where I hoped to be close enough to see where the squirrel headed. Indeed, several minutes later it came scampering along, carrying a nut. Before its next trip, I moved farther along the path, until I saw the squirrel deposit its nut into a hole at the edge of a stump.

There, I found a cache of ten nuts lightly covered by leaves. I replaced the leaves and left the area. When I came back to check an hour later, the nuts were gone. The squirrel had apparently either seen or smelled me and had relocated its nut trove. But I had solved the riddle of how and why there were sometimes clumps of a dozen or more chestnut trees sprouting at the same spot.

How the chestnut seeds are cached may be more relevant to the tree's survival than the location and number of seeds dispersed. Those that I had harvested in the fall were not like those of beans or other seeds, which you can dry and which, after they are rehydrated, will sprout. My chestnut seeds dried quickly indoors but were then dead. I put some outside, where they froze and died as well. Next, I put nuts on moist peat moss and left them unfrozen inside the house. By spring, they were enmeshed in dense white mold, and their contents had turned to mush. How, then, had the bird- and squirrel-cached seeds that overwintered in the woods become seedlings?

Only experiments could answer that question. I enclosed some nuts with a wire screen and placed them on freshly fallen leaves. Others I threw randomly onto leaves. All those protected by the screen died from frost, while those strewn loose onto the leaves disappeared, presumably taken by animals. But I had also buried nuts between five and ten centimeters underground, and these lived through the winter and sprouted seedlings in the spring. I had once seen jays caching acorns by pounding them into soft soil with their bill. Corvids routinely bury food, stick it into crevices, or cover it with nearby debris. Perhaps they did the same with chestnut seeds. Red squirrels put caches of nuts in natural cavities or under layers of leaves on the ground. Apparently, these animals had been more than just dispersers of chestnuts. They were their planters.

The return of the American chestnut tree to our forests may be helped by blue jays and squirrels, but for now our own intervention is also required. The majority of the baby chestnuts that I found were in deep forest shade. In the first year that a seed sprouts, the tiny seedling springs up fifteen to seventeen centimeters, fueled by food stored in the nut. The single, thin, threadlike seedling stalk then bears several leaves to catch whatever sunlight is available. Most of the time, seedlings are overshadowed by large trees and grow only slightly, or not at all. They gather little surplus energy beyond what is required for maintenance or to put out a few more leaves the next year. Nevertheless, their capacity to survive in the shade is impressive. Other forest tree species drop many more seeds, but their seedlings don't survive as long as those of chestnut trees. Most don't even sprout. And like birch trees, chestnuts inherit only a meager startup of energy from their parent trees, and their leaves may be less efficient in energy capture.

Where mottled sunlight illuminates the forest floor, chestnut seedlings may get enough light to capture energy and invest in slow-to-significant growth, but they are highly exposed to predation until they grow beyond the browsing reach of hare, deer, and moose. If, by chance, seedlings are located where openings in the canopy have been created by tree fall, windfall, or logging, sprouts grow at a rate of two or more feet per year and have a good chance of becoming active members of the forest. In twenty to thirty years, they can provide not only offspring but also food and shelter for insects, birds, and mammals. According to a Pennsylvania Game Commission report, "Chestnuts provide wildlife a high-energy food that contains roughly eleven percent protein compared to oaks that average six percent. Chestnuts also contain around sixteen percent fat and forty percent carbohydrates." A mature American chestnut tree can reliably produce as many as six thousand nuts per tree, each year. White oaks produce approximately a thousand nuts per tree, and red oaks about two thousand, but neither family of oaks produces acorns reliably, whereas the chestnut trees flower and produce nuts every year.

The added value of the American chestnut to its habitat explains why there are now active chapters of the American Chestnut Foundation (TACF) in the sixteen states where the tree once reigned. The foundation was begun in 1983 by a group of plant scientists committed to the reestablishment of the tree to its native range. State government agencies are also adopting land management practices with the same objective.

Susceptibility to predation and to fungus is not an all-or-none condition for the species. The trees that were genetically most susceptible are, for the most part, no longer with us, and natural selection is at work in the field, producing more resistant specimens. But given the chestnut's long generation time, the process works slowly. Unfortunately, live chestnut stumps of blight-killed trees still produce shoots, and some of the fungus-susceptible individuals grow large enough to spread their genes, and the disease. The disease is still prevalent, and many of the chestnuts now in the core of its range exist as living stumps.

Maine is at the northern edge of the American chestnut range. Although the state has had a native population of blight-free trees, a young forestry student at the University of Maine in the late 1970s developed a passion for them and a commitment to protect them. Welles Thurber began growing and distributing native chestnut seedlings and scouting chestnuts wherever he went. He became known as "the chestnut guy," similar to James Comp in Michigan. Even before the American Chestnut Foundation was started, Welles met with Frederick Hebard, who became head of TACF's breeding program, and the two of them eventually decided that the best way to preserve Maine's chestnut trees was to work directly with TACF and develop disease-resistant trees. In 1999, the Maine chapter of TACF was formed. Welles started pollinating some native Maine chestnut trees with pollen from TACF's hybrid breeding program. Through a method called backcross breeding, TACF and the Maine chapter of TACF (TMCF) began creating strains that, through multiple generations of breeding, contain some genes from the Chinese chestnut, *Castanea mollissima* — which confers blight resistance — but, after five or six generations, contain mostly genes from the pure American chestnut. Although the Maine chapter uses pollen from hybrid trees, it has adopted a strong position against the use of genetically engineered chestnuts in its program. The Maine chapter is more than halfway toward its goal to plant fifty-four thousand hybrid chestnut trees in its seed orchards by 2020.

None of the state's native American chestnut trees have shown signs of blight at the sixty-seven locations identified by TMCF. A number of those trees are over 75 feet tall, with the tallest — 115 feet — discovered in 2015. It is a thin 50.3 inches in circumference, comparable to the 52 inches of the largest of the trees I planted in 1982. There are several others in Maine that are considerably heftier, and all are healthy.

When I planted my seedlings nearly thirty-four years ago, I had great hope that they would survive. They soon got lost in the shuffle of the vegetation and of my life. Now, from my original twenty-five seedlings, four remain as trees. Hundreds of their offspring grow in the surrounding woods. One of the three largest offspring has reached thirty-one feet in height and has a circumference of ten inches. It grows a few feet taller every year. Individuals thrive, but will the species return to our forests and to our culture? The forests were replete with the American chestnut tree, which grew to splendid proportions. Nobody could imagine that a few microscopic spores would nearly kill it off. Perhaps now, tiny seeds of hope can facilitate its recovery.

The chestnut trees continue to surprise. Two of my Maine trees were badly damaged by porcupines girding them for the bark, and the trees died. Four additional trees that I planted in Vermont at the same time (in 1982) are healthy, but these smaller trees (in shade) are not yet bearing seeds; the four trees originally planted in Maine have been bearing seeds for at least two decades. Pollination is important, and a great variety of insects visit the flowers. When I set out a hive of honeybees near the trees in the spring of 2016, the bees literally swarmed all over the flowers and the trees hummed with their activities. Virtually all the burrs produced viable nuts, an average 2.4 per burr (compared to the 3 possible). In the fall of 2015, for some unexplained reason, the burrs did not open to release their seeds. Blue jays pecked open a few burrs that were partially open and searched widely over the tree crowns, looking for fruit.

Many blue jays "work" a tree at the same time, but only one red squirrel is ever there at once — these animals exhibit strong territoriality. Given a pile of nuts, with some filled and others empty, blue jays hefted the empty ones and then dropped them, and carried off only the filled. As of this writing, in the fall of 2016, the grand-offspring of the originally planted four trees in Maine had produced their first flowers.

• • •

Trees in the forest are in a constant competition with other trees, and different survival strategies have evolved. When I wrote my book *The Trees in My Forest* in 1997, thirteen years after I had planted the American chestnut trees, I did not even put American chestnuts on the list I provided in the book of all the tree species there. The reason was simple: I had not yet allowed myself even a hope that they might survive. Now that they are prospering and reproducing, it is possible to observe their mechanisms, not only of survival, but also of spreading, growing, and competing, all features that are inaccessible to plantation trees.

The forest surrounding the four original chestnut trees is hugely varied in the amount and type of canopy cover. Some of the trees are growing two feet per year, some two inches, and others, such as those under coniferous trees, are in "permanent" shade and are not growing at all. However, all young chestnut trees have a start of around six inches of growth the first year, due to the energy reserves provided in the seed by the parent tree. After that food reserve is exhausted, they need energy input from sunshine or sunlight.

The forest floor is strewn with tree seed. Any one single birch tree, for example, may release (as I have calculated by counting its fruit and seeds per fruit) millions of seeds in only a year, hundreds of millions in a lifetime. Where there is sunlight on open ground, there can be a nearly mosslike carpet of young trees; each lives less than a year. But in the total shade of conifers, there are usually no baby trees whatsoever. None even sprout there except the American chestnuts. It seems amazing to see any tree in total shade, but given the chestnut's investment of resources to get a start, it is perhaps not surprising. What is surprising is that chestnut trees continue to invest and put out leaves for several years. That is, these young trees are amazingly shade-tolerant as they wait for an opportunity to grow, such as when an overshadowing tree is removed and sunlight reaches the ground.

Maturing American chestnut trees match the plasticity of chestnut seedlings, but with a twist. The branches of a swiftly growing chestnut tree are, compared to those of many other forest trees, amazingly shade-*intolerant*. Beeches, the closest relatives of the chestnut trees in this forest (its leaves nearly identical in shape to those of the chestnut), reach out with their branches in all directions, and they keep on growing outward despite being shaded, as if searching laterally for sunshine. Chestnut trees do nothing of the sort: shaded branches whose leaves are no longer gathering energy resources for the tree are no longer supported by the tree — they are shed. They die, rot, and are amputated. Thus, the tree cuts its poor investments and grows ever upward, toward where there is the most light. (It can and does, however, also grow laterally, as do those at the edge of or in my clearing.)

One remarkable outcome of such limb-amputation is a lone American chestnut in Lovell, Maine. It had been publicized widely in the news media — including NPR — as the "tallest American chestnut tree in Maine." It reaches about 115 feet, about three times the height of the tallest of mine. In early December of 2015, Lynn and I drove to see what we expected would be a monster. A guide led us to it, and we would have walked right by it without a second look. In girth it was the same as the ones I had planted. This tree is tall and straight, and all its remaining limbs are now at the top, where it had reached the light, along with equally tall white pines among which it had grown up and still grows. The reason for its shape is obvious: Perhaps a hundred years ago this area had been a field that had seeded in with pines, along with this chestnut. Pines grow fast, and in the trees' competition for direct sunlight, the race had been evenly matched the whole way. The top limbs of this chestnut had always been the most productive, and those below had always been shed and shed again.

It might be construed that the American chestnut is shade-intolerant, but that "intolerance" had here won it a place in a grove among some champion pines. The chestnut's side branches had initially aided its survival, but its straight-and-narrow growth at the top had placed it among the winners of the race to the light.

When the Bough Bends

Natural History, February 1996

A JANUARY THAW IS NOT ALWAYS A WELCOME EVENT IN Maine. If the thaw is accompanied by rain, the woods and roads are soon covered by ice sheets, and people lie low. We wait for the rain to turn back into snow, as it generally does. The storm on January 22, 1995, was by no means as bad as it gets, but I found it particularly annoying. During the night, freezing rain had collected in thick, icy encrustations on the wire screening of my raven research aviary, which collapsed under the weight. In the morning, ice hung like crystal from all the trees — a pretty sight, except that several limbs of my favorite white birch next to the cabin were dangling limply, having snapped from their ice loads. Six-inch-thick gray birch trees were bent over double, their tops touching the ground.

But perhaps more surprising, most of my trees remained intact. Unlike my aviary, a temporary construction of wood and wire, the forest still stood. As I surveyed the icy trees, I began to see them as examples of superior design shaped by evolution; any inferior tree models had long since been obliterated from this landscape by the climate.

Still, some trees do occasionally sustain damage, and this ice storm was severe enough to show up the weaker parts in tree design and to highlight the strengths. I recalled one ice storm about ten years earlier that left the ground in the mature hardwood forests a huge tangle of broken limbs. Gray birches had been broken or had their tips bent all the way to the ground. The white birches, with stronger trunks, had great limbs torn off. But I never saw a limb of a fir or a spruce tree shorn off, and moreover, those trees remained erect in storms. Near my cabin in this latest storm, only the relatively large white and gray birches were affected; the red and sugar maples, American ashes, beeches, yellow birches — all fairly young trees — seemed not to have been damaged at all.

Several days later, when I wandered in a maturing forest nearby, I discovered much more destruction. Many mature seed-bearing oak trees, beeches, maples, white birches, and thick-trunked yellow birches had toppled over, and the ground was littered with their fresh branches. The thick limbs of large pines had also snapped off. While most of the trees were clearly "working" just fine in this particular storm, the broken trees reminded me that I should not take design for granted.

I wondered what principles were at work here. The first of many variables was the amount of ice the limbs had collected. A mere look suggested that the birches had collected more ice than the other hardwoods, so I set out to see if this was the case. With bush cutters, I snipped off five, three- to four-foot-long branches of five different species of young hardwood trees, including white birch. Careful not to knock off any ice, I weighed all twenty-five ice-laden branches with a spring balance — the kind fishermen use to weigh their catch — then spread them out on the floor of the cabin. By late afternoon, the ice had melted, the cabin floor was awash, and I weighed the branches again.

As I had suspected, birch branches collected much more ice than did the branches of the other tree species — dramatically so. On average, birch branches weighed eight times more with their ice load than without it. American ash had the lowest ratio of ice weight to branch weight, while sugar maple, red maple, and apple twigs had an intermediate ratio.

Ash trees have the fewest twigs, which may explain, in part, why they collect the least ice. White birches, which collect more, have bushier and more numerous twigs. Moreover, when birch twigs are partly ice-laden, they tend to droop outward, away from the stem of the tree. Surface tension holds water droplets on the twigs longer, and the slow flow down the twig allows a thin film of ice to form. In contrast, the relatively stiff, horizontal twigs of, for example, apple trees generally hold little ice. The water simply drops off.

The overall architecture of the tree is also important. Ash, maple, and poplar trees (especially younger ones) are shaped roughly like candelabra, and this largely vertical arrangement of twigs has two effects with respect to ice. First, the more a twig points straight up, the less surface it presents to falling rain, and the less water it can intercept. This can be seen in the straight upward-pointing twigs of the American ash. Second, any water that the branches do intercept runs inward toward the trunk (rather than outward, as on the gray birch) and freezes where it can do the least harm. The trunks of most young maples, ashes, and poplars were thickly coated with ice. Possibly this ice even helped stiffen them, rather than weaken them, as it would if it were collected on the outside of branches (as in gray birch). In this particular ice storm, none of the candelabrum-shaped trees showed any sign of being burdened by an ice load, nor did they accumulate much snow later on. This may also help explain why mature trees with large spreading crowns suffer torn limbs more often than do thinner, but more pointed, young trees.

As much as the design of limbs of a northern tree may be shaped in part by selective pressure to minimize ice- and snow-loading, by far the greatest function of the trees' superstructure is to place the leaves to capture sunlight. While necessary for the life of the tree, leaves can also cause its death, and so leaf placement represents a benefits-versus-costs compromise. Without that compromise in mind it may seem counterintuitive that some trees have evolved special enzymes that hasten the leaves' demise, and act to abscise them from the tree after only about three or four months. Shedding serves a variety of functions. For one, it enables a tree to conserve water in dry or desert environments. But the deciduous habit can also be seen as something of an ad hoc solution that allows a maple or birch to survive Maine winters. Ground-hugging shrubs of the far north, such as Labrador tea, bog rosemary, and wintergreen, keep their leaves all winter, proving that winter and leaves are not always incompatible, but tall temperate-zone trees need a line of defense against ice and snow. Last winter in New York City, for instance, ice and snow snapped the limbs of ornamental holly trees (native to more southerly regions) that had broad, evergreen leaves. The two northern native hollies found in Maine — winterberry and mountain holly — shed their leaves and remained undamaged.

Most conifers are marvels of arboreal compromise. While most retain their leaves — needles — in winter, these tend to be erect, stiff, and spiky, and they collect less ice than do broad leaves. This dual capacity of conifers to retain their leaves and still shed ice and snow may be due to their overall shape and strength of limb. An inveterate tree climber since my childhood, I feel qualified to comment on the strength of tree limbs. Neophytes who have climbed with me to the top of a hundred-foot red spruce have watched aghast as I've hung by one hand from, or jumped up and down on, a slender, inch-thick limb of a live spruce. However, jumping on a white pine limb of the same thickness would be suicidal. This northern pine sheds only a proportion of its leaves in the fall, and what it lacks in limb strength it usually makes up in limb thickness. The limbs of tamarack (larch) are even less strong and downright treacherous. If tamarack limbs could accumulate as much ice and snow as spruce and fir limbs do, they would regularly be stripped off the tree. Of course, they almost never are; tamarack is the only northern conifer that is fully deciduous. It sheds all its leaves (needles) in winter.

The main design feature that protects spruce and fir, and to some extent pine, is the very feature that we cherish in them as Christmas trees: their conical shape. Each spring, the trees sprout a single, straight shoot from the top; at the same time, a whorl of three to six branches grows off horizontally, and already existing lower branches stretch even farther to the sides. The number of these umbrella-like tiers of branches, each slightly larger than the one above it, corresponds to the age of the tree.

Conifers do collect snow and ice, and the flow of water is indeed outward, not inward as in the young candelabrum-shaped hardwoods. However, here a new design aspect kicks in and rescues the tree: because they are both highly flexible and tough, the horizontal branches don't break; they bend. As the limbs begin to hang, they support their immense burden not because they are holding it up in the air (as one might hold a bag of cement over one's head) but because they are merely being pulled. That is, they support their load by tensile strength. The "end loading" of the conifer branches is therefore not a liability but an asset. When encumbered by ice and snow, the upper whorls of branches press down and are supported by the lower branches, until a stable cone, or tepeelike structure, is produced.

Pushed inward against the trunk with their weight on the ends, conifer boughs act like a collapsing umbrella; they intercept less precipitation. This is a most desirable trait for a tree in Maine. The more load the trees take on, the more snow slides off, just as it slides off my steep cabin roof or off a tepee. All in all, a conifer's design is the opposite of, say, an American ash's. The ash has few twigs; instead, it grows huge compound leaves that are shed *as if* they were small bushy twigs with many leaves.

The poet Robert Frost was no stranger to the beauties of the forest or of New England winters. This winter when I take measure of my trees, especially my ice-burdened birches, I'll recall his poem "Birches," in which he imagines a boy having swung on these trees (as I so often did as a boy), and writes,

> *But swinging doesn't bend them down to stay*
> *As ice storms do . . .*

O Tannenbaum

Natural History, December 2001–January 2002

ALONG WITH ITS RELIGIOUS SIGNIFICANCE, THE CHRISTMAS season offers those of us who live in northern latitudes a more secular, but also traditional cause to celebrate. We have once again endured the longest nights of the year and can look forward to coasting down on ever-longer days from the winter solstice to spring. To mark this event, people of northern Europe and North America have customarily gone into the forest to cut down a young evergreen tree to bring home.

For my family in New England, the holiday doesn't begin until Christmas Eve. We go into nearby woods where the trees grow thickly, fell a six- to ten-foot spruce or balsam fir, and carry or drag it back to the house. We always select a tree that is not too tall and skinny from struggling to reach the sunlight. We prefer one broad at the base, evenly conical, and well filled in with branches in successive whorls.

While its leaves are still alive and fresh, we traditionally dec-

orate the tree with colorful glass globes, tinsel, red winterberries
from a deciduous holly, spruce and fir cones, and cotton to sim-
ulate snow. The long, thin limbs bend slightly under their ornamental load the same way they bow, rather than break, under ac-
cumulations of snow and ice in the woods. The top is crowned
with a star.

We enjoy choosing our wild tree as much as we do decorat-
ing it. But increasingly, going into the woods to find just the right
specimen is a family ritual out of reach for most people. While
city dwellers and suburbanites can make an annual tradition of
selecting and purchasing a tree from a vendor, I wonder if this may
lead us to forget what an authentic evergreen looks like. Farmed
Christmas trees can be manicured with clips or power saws into
any desired shape. Ironically, the shape that is most in demand
in a commercial tree (one now generally grown not in a forest) is
what we think a Christmas tree is supposed to look like when left
to grow on its own. That is, the trees are pruned in an attempt
to improve on nature. To me, that seems somewhat like painting
roses red.

An unaltered conifer is unmistakable if one is aware of how its
shape is achieved naturally. And a tree's shaping starts at the top.
By late summer and on through fall and winter, each fir, spruce,
or pine is topped by a single pencil-like vertical twig bearing a
cluster of buds. This twig is the "leader" that will eventually become a one-year's growth section of the trunk of the tree. (The
trunk below the young leader consists of a series of previous annual leaders.) Any bud — or any twig resulting from it — has the
potential to become a leader, but usually only the centermost one
will assume leadership, while the buds on the sides of the same
top cluster will end up becoming a whorl of horizontal branches.

How these decisions are made is a matter of physiological checks and balances that involve a host of plant hormones interacting in response to the position of the tree in the forest and to resources such as light.

The leader releases auxins, hormones that work in conjunction with others called gibberellins, to promote its elongation while at the same time inhibiting the growth of nearby buds and twigs. This shunting of resources to the leader is known as "apical dominance," and without it an evergreen would burgeon equally in all directions. In a shaded forest, where each young tree competes with thousands of other seedlings, indiscriminate growth would be suicidal. The trees next to it, growing conically and relatively straight up, would rob it of light. The only way any one conifer can survive the competition — and only a tiny percentage do — is to come to a narrow point at the top and to extend sideways only secondarily. The tree's priority is to allocate energy to the leader so that the whole organism can outstretch the other trees in the race toward the light.

Leadership, however, is not irreversible. Changes occur routinely, due for the most part to deer or moose nipping off the succulent tops of young trees (in winter I have also seen red squirrels feeding specifically on the leader buds, possibly because they are the largest) or to breakage caused by storms and fallen branches. In such cases, one might expect chaotic growth in all directions, but a corrective mechanism kicks in.

In a tree left leaderless and with newly uninhibited lateral growth, several shoots from the top cluster reach upward and engage in a competition until one of them becomes the new leader. It is a slow process, taking a few years to complete. Eventually, as one or another of the contenders gets a slight upper hand, so to speak, it produces more auxins than the others do, and these accumulate on the twig's lower side, causing the cells there to elongate. This favored twig then bends toward the vertical to take on the role of leader. The coniferous symmetry is restored, and the tree can then again stretch skyward and compete with its evergreen neighbors.

A commercial Christmas tree starts out like any other conifer, but the tips of both its leader and lateral branches are clipped off. Such trimming removes the growth inhibition of buds and twiglets farther in on the branch. The trees then direct less energy upward than outward and become bushier. With its natural branching patterns disrupted, the tree is, strictly speaking, no longer a wild specimen. To a pagan purist like me, that spoils the effect. The evergreen tree, once symbolic of forest wildness, has been tamed into a bush.

Should I care if this representation of the natural world that we bring into our living room is altered to suit human expectations? Probably not. But we may come to prefer and even insist on a domesticated tree with the "perfect" shape, a tree we would never see in nature. Which leads me to wonder: If our ignorance of how conifers grow can allow us to do this to a Christmas tree, how much more might we alter nature at large without caring, or even knowing?

INSECTS

Reading Tree Leaves

Natural History, December 2016–January 2017

A TIGER SWALLOWTAIL CATERPILLAR (*Papilio canadensis*) was perched on a leaf of a hickory seedling I had planted alongside the path to our cabin. It would normally have been easy to miss because it was bright green. But this was mid-August, and the caterpillar's bright green showed up against the leaves that were starting to turn yellow with a tinge of orange.

This individual caterpillar soon became familiar because I saw it every day. To my eventual surprise I noticed it always on the same leaf, in the same place on it, and in the same posture. Yet it seemed to be getting larger by the day.

This went on for about a week. *Did it feed at night?* I wondered. To find out I got up near midnight to check — and there in the beam of my flashlight, it was still perched precisely as it had been during the day. This proved nothing, of course, because one check one night versus dozens in the day does not count for much, so I checked once more that moonless night, and there it was, crawling along the leaf petiole, straight to the end of one of the foot-long compound leaves, to feed on the end of the terminal leaflet where there were already signs of previous feeding. It fed for five minutes, turned around, and in apparent haste crawled back to its usual resting place on the distant leaf. Next, it turned to face in the direction from which it had come, defecated a small dark pellet, and then remained motionless.

Apparently, this caterpillar fed at night on distant leaves, and came back to rest in the day at the same spot on the specific leaf. But why did it feed at night? Was it to avoid predators such as birds that would detect it by movement during the day? Its green color on normally green backgrounds might support the idea that it hides from predators, in which case movement would reveal it to predators. A single observation had demonstrated that it feeds at night. But dozens of times seeing it in the same place in the day did not disprove that it fed in the day also. If it always fed just briefly at widely spaced times, then I might have been lucky to have seen it feed at all, night or day. I was intrigued enough to examine this caterpillar's behavior more systematically, over successive days. It then revealed itself.

Day and night, at about three-hour intervals, the caterpillar sallied forth from its usual perch on the same leaf to travel to other leaves and feed from those. Its traveling time out was about two minutes one way. It fed for about five minutes, then immediately returned to its perch. Such a schedule allowed about a one-in-twenty-five chance for me to see it off its perch and feeding at any one random time in the thirteen hours of daylight that I might look for it to be feeding. Curiously, it usually took several successive feeding trips to the same leaf as well, making me wonder why it did not stay to feed right where it was. Why leave, and expose itself by movement, if only to come back to the same place? Was that place special?

After each feeding trip, when the caterpillar returned, it turned around from the tip on the (slanting) leaf to again face in the same direction for the next trip. Turning around and assuming the resting position took only a few seconds. However, after one foraging, I observed this caterpillar spend forty minutes waving its outstretched body back and forth and up and down the leaf at its resting place, and also turning around twice more before finally assuming its usual resting position. During the whole time, its head appeared to be brushing over the leaf surface all around itself. I suspected it was coating the leaf with silk, but with the naked eye I could not see any silk. Nevertheless, I took photographs, and they showed a glint of thin fibers on the leaf, corroborating my impression. Some caterpillars, such as tent caterpillars and fall webworms, build communal webs of silk that serve as shelters for safety and keeping warm. But this was no web. It was an almost invisible covering of the leaf surface. The swallowtail caterpillar perched on a thin layer of almost invisible silk, where it became possibly more visible rather than less, and in addition it exposed itself by its travel between that resting area and where it fed.

Whatever its silk pad does for the caterpillar, it must have a benefit, or the physiology of making the silk, and the behaviors of applying it to the leaf and traveling to and from it, would not have evolved. It was puzzling but distinctive behavior, and it awakened pleasant memories of caterpillar magic of long ago, which might provide insights.

I have hunted and raised caterpillars, some of which I remember as individuals because of their rarity and distinctive appearance. None did anything like this. There was the one Io moth caterpillar — green with red stripes along its sides — that I found as a boy on a low bush in our field on the farm in Maine, and the two (one brown, one green) four-horned sphinx moth caterpillars found on an elm tree. Mostly I had the usual Luna, Cecropia, and Polyphemus, and various sphinx moths, nuctuids, notodontids, and also a variety of butterfly larvae, including swallowtails. The caterpillars I found and raised were beautiful and undemanding, and provided the magic of a prize to come.

Caterpillar of a sphinx moth, Manduca sexta, *that I sketched as found, feeding on jimsonweed in the Mojave Desert in California.*

As a doctoral student at UCLA I raised caterpillars of one species only, the tobacco sphinx moth, *Manduca sexta*. They are pests to tobacco farmers in the South, and tomato farmers almost everywhere loathe them. Having seen them in Maine in our garden, I was excited to find them in the searing Mojave Desert in California. They there fed on the native trumpet flower plants, *Datura stramonium*, also called jimsonweed and locoweed, known for its fatal toxicity and as a powerful hallucinogen to humans.

The tobacco moth caterpillars had obviously breached the plants' biochemical defenses. I often found several of them, each weighing as much as a chickadee, on the same low plant that might not have very many green leaves to begin with. The jimsonweed plants were scattered widely, hundreds of meters apart, making it unlikely that after a caterpillar had eaten one plant, it could traverse the hot sands to find another.

How could the caterpillars survive to remain thick, and plump, and hydrated in dry desert heat and sunshine? I was a beginning graduate student in need of a thesis project, and worked determinedly for a year trying to find what I hoped would be a new-to-science physiological mechanism of water conservation. I failed to find anything of the sort, even though I had a micro-balance at my disposal, with which I measured the caterpillars' weight loss in real time at different temperatures and humidity right in front of my eyes, on a moving strip chart. But when they started moving, water loss instantly shot up, and when they were off their plant being measured in the heat they always kept moving, so I had no idea what their water loss might be in their normal behavior of perching on their food plant, when water loss from that of the plant could not be isolated. Also, relative humidity was difficult to control, plus they defecated often. I gave up on the project, failing to find what I wanted to find. But in retrospect, perhaps a secret to the caterpillars' success was in plain sight, in their behavior.

In the desert the caterpillars fed on the *Datura* leaves by staying almost always under them, and using them as a sunshade. This buffered them from direct solar input and presumably also reduced water loss by reducing convection. To examine more closely their leaf-handling behavior with respect to leaf shape, I raised caterpillars on easy-to-grow tobacco leaves, allowing me to present them with leaves of various sizes and shapes. I was surprised to see that when they were attached to the petiole at the leaf base of either a large ovate leaf or a thin long one, they consumed the entire leaf, which was usually several times longer than their own body length. They did so without moving from the spot and without wasting or dropping any part of it, while at the same time keeping the uneaten part of the leaf over them like an umbrella as a shield from the direct rays of the sun. The key to their behavior was simple: while remaining clamped tightly to the leaf petiole with their rear claspers, they used their three pairs of pro-legs to "walk" their front end forward on the leaf, starting to feed only after reaching the most distant part, the leaf tip, and only then consuming the leaf back to the base where they remained attached. While the leaves are the caterpillars' only water source, they fed on them prudently, while also using them for shelter from the sun and thus a guard against desiccation.*

I published the mechanics of the caterpillars' feeding behavior in the premier journal *Animal Behavior* — my first publication about any animal behavior. But the real prize proved to be from the by-catch; the moths that came from the caterpillars led to the discovery of a new physiological mechanism whereby some other

---

* At any point, a project may seem like a failure. It took me two years to find out that I could not distinguish whether a *Manduca sexta* hornworm caterpillar is feeding to maintain water balance in a hot, dry desert environment or feeding for growth. This led to other questions instead, this time about the sphinx moths that came from them — and then I was led to my eventual breakthrough papers about insect thermoregulation; see "Hot- and Cold-Blooded Moths."

insects regulate their body temperature. In my great excitement about the story coming from that discovery, and the numerous doors it opened, I forgot caterpillars for years.

The story of how caterpillars eat leaves and what it means in their lives was revived by a stray observation of tree leaves at the University of Minnesota Experiment Station at Itasca. I happened to be there under a basswood tree that had limbs over a cleared walkway, and there on the ground were several fresh green leaves. It was July. There had been no storm, and in any case green leaves don't just drop off the trees. Examining them, I saw that one side of each had a missing crescent, leaving a smooth, not toothed, edge. A closer look revealed, even more surprisingly, that most of the leaf petiole was missing as well; leaves never get shed by the petiole breaking because the petiole is the most fibrous part of the leaf. The indirect evidence was telling: a caterpillar had first eaten on and then *discarded* the partially eaten leaves. I then found the caterpillar. It was an underwing (*Catocala*) moth caterpillar. I watched and photographed it as it fed on a leaf, backed up to chew through the thick woody petiole, and then crawled off to hide, camouflaged against a branch. After resting and digesting, it then repeated the behavior for its next meal, at another leaf.

What I had so long not noticed, I now see routinely. Any cleared path through a forest of deciduous trees shows such leaves of many tree species shed by caterpillars of all kinds, including those of many sphinx moths, but excluding the tobacco sphinx.

A caterpillar feeding on a tree, unlike the *Manduca* moth caterpillar on jimsonweed in the desert, incurs essentially no cost in food loss by "wasting" leaf tissue because there is almost always another leaf available nearby. However, there is no nutrition in the woody petiole, and chewing through it takes time and effort, so that cost must buy something. We now know that the benefit may be huge — it may save the caterpillar's life. Experiments and observations with birds show, surprisingly, that they may, as I had myself in caterpillar hunting, cue in on leaf damage to locate caterpillars that may otherwise be nearly invisible because of their excellent mimicry of inedible objects, such as bark, twigs, and even parts of the leaf. Conversely, in the arms race between caterpillars and birds, birds have evolved counter-strategies. Blue jays and chickadees in the lab and in field conditions have been shown to learn not only to associate food with the feeding damage caused by caterpillars* but also to differentiate leaf damage created by the browse of palatable versus unpalatable caterpillars. An alternative hypothesis has been suggested — that the caterpillars are instead getting rid of leaves they have scented by feeding on them, to avoid attracting parasitoids. However, the caterpillars that are unpalatable to birds do not need to disguise their feeding damage. To the contrary, these conspicuous caterpillars with hairs, spines, and bright colors are fast-moving, non-hiding, day-feeding messy eaters, leaving leaf tatters behind. For such caterpillars the advantage of getting rid of the feeding evidence may or may not result

---

* The comparison of the behavior alone precluded a palatable versus unpalatable parasitical hypothesis. But I wanted proof that this had been the agent in natural selection of the feeding behavior — Scott Collins and I got it in a study conducted years later in a large aviary at my cabin in Maine, with wild-caught chickadees, *Parus atricapillus*. In experiments using small deciduous trees, some with and some without damaged leaves on them, we determined that the chickadees learned to search selectively in trees with leaf damage if they had previously found food on others with similarly damaged leaves. Subsequently, in collaboration with other researchers, we showed that blue jays learn to distinguish the difference between screen-projected images of leaves damaged and undamaged by caterpillars. They additionally distinguish between those fed on by edible versus unpalatable caterpillars.

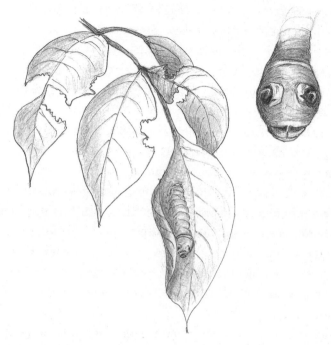

Tiger swallowtail caterpillar on its resting spot; it usually fed at some distance from that spot. The close-up at right is not its head but the anterior of its body, which mimics a snake's head.

in benefits, but does not exceed the cost of the effort enough to be a potent selective pressure.

The caterpillars of the tiger swallowtail that I was watching at our Maine cabin feed on trees — typically black cherry, poplar, birch, and apple. Unlike the *Manduca*, which feeds on herbs, they should be able to clip off leaves without suffering a penalty of food loss. Nevertheless, they had to solve the problem of predation, as other caterpillars have. The caterpillar I watched demonstrated a hint of that behavior. It fed without the least interruption as the wind-whipped leaves rocked and swiveled in all sorts of ways. Yet although it did not respond to my visual presence anywhere around it, whenever I touched the branch, it hunched up into the defensive posture. Such discrimination should allow it to detect a bird or predatory insect landing near it, causing movements distinct from those created by the wind.

Caterpillars respond to the threat of predation in many ways, including patterns of movement and changes to physical appearance, and tiger swallowtail caterpillars too have varied strategies. When still very small, they are white with gray markings, and closely mimic bird droppings. After their third molt, when they are luminescent green, they have a bulbous front end, which sports a pair of remarkably eyelike decorations, and they respond to a mild alarm by tucking their head under their front end to mimic a green snake's head. The pair of fake eyes greatly enhances that effect.

The snake-image effect is well represented in both morphology and back-up behavior in other caterpillars, including sphinx moths. This display is different, dependent on origins: the "snake head" disguise can be either on caterpillars' front or hind end. The snake fake is therefore likely to be of several evolutionary origins. In the tiger swallowtail larva, the fake-snake response is enhanced by the extrusion of a forked, light-colored, fleshlike papilla that resembles a forked tongue, an option that may be unique to swallowtail larvae.

The everted "flicking tongue" prongs, called osmeteria, are not just a visual effect used as a psychological deterrent for snake-wary birds. They are also associated with a chemical defense likely aimed at other predators. Caterpillars are prime prey for many insect parasites and predators, for whom a chemical defense is effective, and the osmeteria, when everted, deliver a chemical arsenal like a witch's brew of poisonous foul odors. It contains, out of a long list of documented chemicals, monoterpene hydrocarbons, sesquiterpenic compounds, a mixture of aliphatic acids and esters. The chemicals repel ants, spiders, and mantids. We find them irritating as well, and I suspect a blue jay or vireo that grabs one of these caterpillars would immediately associate the snakelike appearance with the real threat of chemical irritation.

The tiger swallowtail caterpillar did not remove or minimize its feeding damage, even though it fed on tree leaves. It therefore seems unlikely that the tiger swallowtail retreats to its silk pad when not feeding in order to distance itself from feeding damage. Perching on the leaf in the sun, as northern swallowtail caterpillars do, would both enhance solar heating and reduce convective cooling, thereby allowing them to maintain an elevated body temperature, which would speed digestion and the rate of growth. Few caterpillars can do that because tree leaves, including those the swallowtail caterpillars normally feed on — such as cherry, ash, and birch — have a shiny and hard surface. To stay on leaves, most caterpillars need to clamp onto the petiole or the leaf-edge. Perhaps the swallowtail caterpillar's silk pad gives it the means for a strong foothold on top of the leaf, so it won't get dislodged from the tree in a storm. Of course I don't know that, because it has not been tested, but I am sure that the production of silk is not just a random thing without some function. One can't always know how the tiger got its stripes, but one can try to find out what the stripes do for the tiger.

Hot- and Cold-Blooded Moths

Previously published as "False Assumptions: A Matter of Degrees," *Natural History*, October 2015

IT LOOKED LIKE A SMALLISH HUMMINGBIRD, BUT IT WAS A Nessus sphinx moth, one of forty-five species of North American sphinx moths. What caught my attention more than anything else were the two brilliant hornetlike yellow bands across the dark back of its abdomen, contrasting with the delicate patterns of chocolate brown and cinnamon. The Nessus — which continues to feed after the caterpillar stage, as do some but not all sphinx moths — has converged to look uncannily like a hummingbird, although the one I saw near my cabin in western Maine could have stood in also for a hybrid with a hornet. The Nessus is not only hummingbird-like in the proportion of its short plump body and small propeller-like wings, but it has a birdlike short tail at the tip of its abdomen, and, unlike most sphinx moths, it is day-active. The most startling feature of the sphinx moth is its "tongue."

The long rigid bill of a hummingbird has evolved to access nectar in generally long tubular flowers. The bill, as with other birds', is formed by the upper and lower jaw (or maxilla and mandible). In moths, the equivalent to a bird's bill is the proboscis, which is derived from a pair of maxillae; in most insects these serve as the laterally moving mouthparts that bite and chew. But moths, unlike bees and hummingbirds, have no tongue housed between the two maxillae. Instead, the maxillae have been modified to abut permanently against each other to form an interlocking tube that has become a sucking straw. Some sphinx moths that do not feed as adults lack this structure, while others that feed from flowers in the same way that hummingbirds do have maxillae that are as much as three and a half times their body length.

The long tonguelike tube enables some moths to reach nectar that is even beyond the reach of hummingbirds. Apparently, for hummingbirds the potential benefit of reaching nectar with a bill sticking out a foot or more ahead of them comes at too great a cost. It would likely have been too costly for moths too, except that they have an added ability: they can curl this whole feeding mechanism into a tight mass, tuck it under their "chin" until needed, extend it in an instant, and then manipulate it with pinpoint accuracy. This highly evolved mechanism is extremely unlikely ever to be matched by hummingbirds, because both taxa are too far along with their own specializations. Selective pressure can act on only what already exists. Each specialization can be improved upon but not changed to a new design. These moths have evolved to converge on hummingbirds because they both feed on nectar from flowers, which have also evolved in response to them — all three have been engaged in a coevolutionary arms race for a very long time.

In 1862, while Charles Darwin was studying orchids, he received specimens of *Angraecum sesquipedale*, an orchid that had been discovered in Madagascar in 1798. He was impressed by its

My sketch of white-lined shaking moths, Hyles lineata, *which I observed taking nectar of Chuparosa* (Beloperone californica) *flowers while at very high muscle temperatures on a cool evening in the Anza-Borrego Desert.*

very long nectary — the tube leading from the flower entrance to the nectar — and predicted a sphinx moth must pollinate the plant. He was ridiculed at the time, but in 1903 he was vindicated when such a moth was discovered in Madagascar by the naturalists Lionel Walter Rothschild (Lord Baron) and Karl Jordan of the Tring Museum in London. That species of large sphinx moth was named *Xanthopan morganii praedicta.*

Darwin's insight into what pollinated the orchid was based on the morphology of the plant and that of sphinx moths. The underlying energy exchange driving the pollination — the energetics or biological thermodynamics — was not yet understood. The plant as it evolved needed to invest in the production of fuel in the form of nectar/sugar to attract and reward pollinators. Nectar/sugar, however, is a food desired by all sorts of animals that could eagerly take all the nectar and not pollinate, and the resulting low nectar stores could discourage or eliminate other animals that could potentially be pollinators. The plant, therefore, needed to invest also in a nectary tube that was long enough to exclude nectar thieves and reward pollinators.

The longer the nectar tube got, the more exclusive became the pollinator clientele. It was crucial that the flower reliably provided what its corolla's shape, color, or scent advertised; otherwise, the pollinator would learn to ignore the signs. The longer the nectar tube, the more food energy would be available exclusively for the pollinator, and the more available nectar created a more energy-dependent pollinator. On the other hand, more energy enabled sphinx moths to be selected for larger size and longer tongues, and it also facilitated both hovering and long-distance flight. That is, pollination of widely scattered plants became energetically feasible for long-distance flying moths. However, their very long tongues did put sphinx moths at a disadvantage in competing for the small amount of nectar in flowers with short corollas, which are ideally suited for shorter-tongued insects.

An added unknown in Darwin's time were the roles of physiology, heat production, and body temperature regulation that are also important variables in understanding the pollinator-plant equation. The activities of insects — as with all animals — depend on muscle contractions. And muscle contractions produce heat.

Insects have been commonly categorized as cold-blooded, even though some were found that could elevate their body temperature. Early in my career, during a research study in 1969, I was astounded when I measured the muscle temperature of white-lined sphinx moths, *Celerio* (now *Hyles*) *lineata,* that were hovering at flowers on a cold evening in the Anza-Borrego Desert of California. The first individual that I captured and stuck with a thermocouple registered 44 degrees Celsius (or 111.4 degrees F), certainly not cold-blooded by our human standard of a normal body temperature of around 37 degrees C.*

Hot-bloodedness in insects is, as in vertebrate animals, both an immediate consequence of their activity and an ultimate necessity for it. Muscles heat up due to the heat produced as a byproduct of contracting, and they must be adapted to operate at near the temperature that they have been subjected to during activity over the time course of their evolutionary history. Thus, prior to activity, large moths and other large insects must now shiver to be able to fly. Size is of critical importance.

A large-bodied animal loses heat passively only slowly in comparison to a small one. Furthermore, at a given body size — all other things like insulation being equal — the cooling rate is in direct proportion to the temperature difference between the object and the environment. Sphinx moths are relatively large; they contract their massive flight muscles thirty to sixty times per second; they are active in the summer, and they are most common in tropical climes. They are therefore more hot-blooded

---

* This discovery was startling and unexpected because insects were known largely as cold-blooded animals, and therefore perhaps less developed than "highly" developed animals, birds, and mammals. It set my research path for the next twenty years on a new and productive trajectory.

from their own metabolism than most animals, and they share with us humans some common thermally related problems and traits.

We evolved in a hot environment where we were burdened with internal heat production from vigorous sustained heat production during the chase for food. We evolved a superb mechanism of dumping excess body heat by sweating. Some insects have also evolved the ability to stabilize (regulate) their body temperature to get rid of excess body heat, instead of simply reducing their rate of heat production, that is, energy output.

Some desert cicadas exude liquid from glands on their body, which cools them when they engage in their highly muscular activity of singing. The liquid for this "sweating" comes indirectly from the juices of plants that get water through their deep underground roots. Honeybees have a different twist: they regurgitate nectar and let it evaporate from their tongue like a dog, or spread it with their forelegs over their thorax if it gets overheated. Sphinx moths, as I found out, can do neither, but have anatomy and physiology that puts them on an equal footing with a warm-blooded animal, not just in the practical but also in the literal sense, in that they shunt the excess heat generated by their working flight muscles to their abdomen, which acts like a heat radiator of a car to keep the engine from overheating.

Some species of mostly night-flying noctuids, or owlet moths, are specialized to be active in early winter and spring, presumably because they then escape predation by birds. Their thermal problem is precisely the opposite of sphinx moths' because they are much smaller and because air temperatures are sometimes near the freezing point of water when they fly. Anatomy, it turns out, plays a huge role in these moths' ability to retain most of their heat in the thorax, where the flight muscles reside, and to prevent it from leaking out. They have fluffy insulation on the thorax as well as two counter-current heat exchangers, one that reduces heat loss to the head and another that nearly prevents it from leaking into the abdomen, thereby retaining it in the thorax to keep the flight muscles operating. However, other smaller winter-flying moths, some species of the family Geometridae, are so small, they can barely heat up at all. They have evolved an entirely different strategy to solve the same problem of flight muscle operation.

We routinely see these other "winter moths" in our headlights if we drive through a wooded area in October and November. Amazingly, they fly with a body temperature almost the same as the air temperature, even down to the freezing point of water. How is that possible? The answer is, again, that their muscles are adapted to the temperature they experience, but they are limited in energy output. They have large wings that act in part as sails, and their very light bodies require minimal work to stay airborne. These moths do not generate much heat, and could not retain most of it even if they did. Interestingly, every one we will ever see in our headlights will be a male. Why? Because the females lack wings. They are grublike in form, and rotund from their load of eggs.

I mention these innovations of insects because, given their generally small body size, the enormous exercise that they are capable of, and the harsh environments of heat and cold where they can be active, it seems more impressive to me that many regulate a higher body temperature than our own, and do it amazingly well, compared to our own supposed superiority of evolution as warm-blooded animals. This does not mean that most insects are not at most times cold-blooded. Their matching of body temperature to their environment is standard for all, even the most hot-blooded. Like the relaxation of body temperature practiced by most vertebrate animals, it usually serves as an adaptation for energy economy.

The amazing thing about insects is not what most of them may do most of the time. It is what some can do at some times. To ignore these variations is like presuming that hominids can move only by walking because statistically — at almost any time — that is the most common method of locomotion.

Woolly and Wondrous

Natural History, February 2016

IN EARLY NOVEMBER, I SAW A DOT DRIFTING AND HOVERING around me. It shone white against the dark forest background. There was not a breath of wind, but the dot was moving to the right, to the left, up, down. Mesmerized by this shiny white speck that was obviously self-propelled, I looked around and saw another, and another, and after some minutes, yet another. Because of my proximity, I knew they were much smaller than the noctuid moths that fly at night or the frail geometrid moths that flutter weakly both at night and in the day at this time of year. They were too small for me to see if they had wings, but by their behavior I concluded they did; they could only be insects. I waited for others to come near and succeeded in grabbing three. There was not much to see in my hand afterward, only tiny wings and a small stain of dark mush — enough, however, for me to know that they were aphids. But their flying in November, when there is frost every night and the chance of snow, seemed odd.

Their whiteness indicated they might be woolly alder aphids

(*Prociphilus tessellatus*), covered with their delicate slender filaments of white wax, and I soon came across clusters of them attached to alder twigs, each resembling a cushion of snow, or perhaps a mushroom or mold infecting their twig. Within clusters,
aphids are closely packed together and spend all winter on twigs
exposed to the elements. In the summer, the aphids are protected
by ants that milk them for honeydew by stroking them with their
antennae, which causes the aphids to release an anal secretion that
is a filtrate of plant juices. Aphids need amino acids to make protein, but when they suck juice from twigs, they also imbibe a surplus
of sugar that is not needed for their low-energy, sessile lives, spent
effectively glued to one spot generation after generation.

For as long as I can remember, I have routinely seen the white
patches of seemingly comatose aphid colonies stuck to alder tree
twigs, and I've paid them little attention. But the white, cottony,

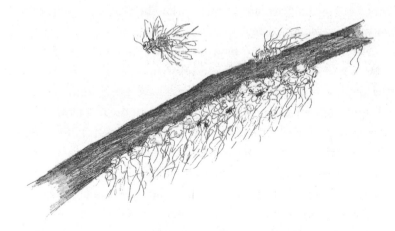

*Woolly aphid colony of about forty individuals aggregated on the under-
side of a twig, along with numerous nymphs among them (four shown).
All adults are covered in white wax filaments, including the one winged
form shown in flight.*

winged forms that were wafting about me in November provided
a glimpse into what might be an exciting story.

I brought my now-valued specimens — three squashed aphids
carefully placed in a piece of notepaper in my pocket — back as
treasure to my cabin, along with a twig I had found that a colony
had attached to. With a magnifying glass I could verify that the flying objects were indeed two-winged aphids. I half expected others
to emerge from the colony and start flying after they warmed up,
but I kept the colony in the cabin for a day, and nothing budged.
When I disassembled it, peeling away the white, stringy wax covering, a colony of fifteen round squat blobs was revealed. Each
one was a wingless dark-blue aphid with legs so tiny, they could
not possibly be useful, even for crawling. These aphids were huge
in comparison to the winged forms I had caught the day before. I
also found twenty-two almost microscopic wingless nymphs. They
were tucked into the interstices among the adult aphids. The babies were probably recently born (or hatched) and overwintering
within the colony.

The colony seemed to be a home that may help protect the
young, and possibly give them a head start in the spring. All of
the big, round, wingless aphids must have been adult females,
who throughout summer and early fall were the colony mothers,
participants in the curious asexual (parthenogenetic) life cycle of
aphids. After many generations of virgin births, however, aphids
produce nymphs that undergo a physiological change: they grow
wings and become sexual. Changes in the environment may trigger the response — shorter days, cooler temperatures, or reduced
food supply. It was these seldom-encountered winged and sexual
aphids that I had seen and caught.

The winged aphids may not have issued from the colony I found
— but they would have been from one like it and were probably

born several weeks earlier. They had been, and maybe still were, looking for mates or a place to overwinter, and, if female, possibly looking for another alder on which to attach and become a colony mother, ready to restart the life cycle in the spring. That is the story of such aphids.

I might have let it go at that. But then I realized something odd. The colony that I had pulled apart on this November day already contained a batch of babies (perhaps the next generation of asexuals), and the winged (final sexual and dispersal) forms were simultaneously present in the field. Those nymphs, to come to maturity next spring, would not be able to disperse. They would perhaps remain attached to the alder twig where their mothers, and their grandmothers, and their great-grandmothers, had grown up. This means that the colony is not an ephemeral entity; it is a multiyear community, which periodically sends out sexual propagules to establish colonies elsewhere. Why could the woolly aphids not be like other aphids, semi-communal at times, simply from the incidental clumping due to adults' parthenogenetic reproduction at the same spot? These aphids were clumped into an apparently deliberate tight package, which was all the more a community because the dense cover of white wax obscured the individuals. I had routinely seen these white-covered aphid colonies in past winters, never suspecting they contained nymphs.

Spurred on by my find of what would normally be the end of the annual aphid cycle, I had a newfound interest in woolly aphids. The next day, I kept my eyes open for colonies. With the search image in my mind, I almost immediately found one colony after another — a total of thirty-two. A pattern jumped out. Although only one colony generally occupied each clump of alder bushes, there was often another colony close by. In one of my finds, the alder bush had ten colonies. Based on the six colonies that I picked apart, the number of aphids per colony ranged widely, from 9 to 213. None contained winged forms but all contained approximately twice as many nymphs as adult females. All of the nymphs were of the same, almost microscopic, size. These observations reinforced the notion that colonies grow over a timespan much longer than just one season. But why do they persist? Does the white fluffy wax have something to do with the pattern? For this unusual wax to have evolved, it must provide some advantage to the aphids. What could it be?

The fact that the wax hides the plump aphids is probably not incidental. I saw no evidence that any colony had been ripped apart. The white material may indeed be perceived to be so different from birds' usual prey that it is ignored. And if not, and a bird did pick at an aggregation, it would first taste wax and be put off. I licked an aggregation: the wax was flavorless and unlikely to be toxic. However, that it offers protection from predation is shown indirectly by the caterpillars and lacewings that have evolved to prey on aphids within the colony — they use the wax to camouflage themselves.

It may seem ironic that the highly conspicuous wax, which makes the woolly aphid colony easy to spot, would be a defense against predators. Charles Darwin had pondered why prey species are sometimes so eye-catching, and it had long been an enigma. We now see eye-catching coloration as aposematic, or warning — just as bright and colorful markings distinguish noxious insects, which a predator will soon learn to avoid, the bright white may serve as a reminder that aphids do not taste good. Alternatively, when seen from a distance, the white may mimic snow or mold, which does not warrant a second look. But I am glad I did take a second look to find something intriguing: both baby and parent woolly aphids in colonies, along with flying ones, in November.

Winter Guests

Natural History, February 2001

EVEN BEFORE I FINISHED BUILDING THE CABIN, I COULD SEE that it had potential. Bubo, my tame great horned owl, perched on one of the rafters rather than staying out in the woods, where the blue jays harassed it. Similarly, as soon as I crossed the doorstep, the June hordes of bloodsucking black flies and horseflies left off their hot pursuit. Aside from harboring a few stray houseflies in late summer, the cabin was a sanctuary. When winter came to the Maine woods, however, it became more appealing to the wild local fauna, and many adopted my haven as their own. As a first-time log cabin builder, I had made many construction mistakes, and the biggest was not anticipating the entrance of winter guests — thousands of them.

Among mammals, my annual visitors include a few common smoky shrews, short-tailed shrews, red-backed voles, and last but certainly not least in numbers, deer mice. As far as I'm concerned, all are welcome except the cutest of the lot, the deer mice. Normally, deer mice spend winter in tree holes and other crevices,

Bubo, my tame great horned owl.

where they build cozy nests and stay warm by huddling in groups. Since I built the cabin, I've done my best to plug every conceivable opening with oakum, a sisal fiber more often used to stop holes in wooden boats, but deer mice seem to penetrate the cabin easily. The mice apparently gain entry through tiny apertures or create openings by pulling out the oakum plugs between the logs. In this they are aided by the larger and stronger flying squirrels that use the oakum for lining their winter nests in natural tree holes or in birdhouses that I provide, primarily for other occupants.

On any winter night I can hear mobs of deer mice scampering overhead in the space between the metal roofing and a sheet of insulating Styrofoam. At intervals their footsteps stop and I hear them crunching into the Styrofoam. White Styrofoam flakes stream down like snow over the bed and floor. Once inside, the mice shred clothing for their nests, leave peanuts in my bed, and burrow into the dry goods. The possibility that they might carry disease tweaks at the back of my mind too. If I set traps, I commonly catch up to four mice in a night, but there are always many more that have the run of the place. The joint efforts of the deer mice and the flying squirrels also appear to provide the main means of entrance for "the crowd."

The crowd is always snug inside, come winter. It consists mostly of cluster flies. According to Harold Oldroyd, who wrote the fly bible, the 1964 *Natural History of Flies*, there are several species of these robust flies of the genus *Pollenia*. Most of them are several times the size of houseflies. *Pollenia* are calliphorid, or "flesh" flies. The larvae of our native species eat the flesh of dead animals, but the main species in the cabin, *Pollenia rudis*, was introduced from Europe, and their larvae parasitize live earthworms. Big and bristly, these flies are not handsome, in contrast to the metallic green or gun-barrel blue of our native blowflies (which never enter the cabin at all).

In the fall *P. rudis* crowd on the logs outside the cabin and sun themselves. When it starts to get cool, they slip through the cracks. By November most of them have made their way inside, but they remain unobtrusive unless I build a roaring fire in the wood stove. Then they come pouring out of all the crevices and, in an hour or so, if it is still daylight, gather by the thousands in buzzing masses at each of the eight windows, making a collective hiss. They apparently perceive the warmth as the return of spring, and take it as their signal to leave by flying directly to the light at the windows. Even on the coldest days, if I open the windows, they rush out and fly a short distance before the cold grips them and they become immobilized and fall on or into the snow. The chickadees have a feast. When subjected to the cold of a Maine winter, these flies are physiologically equipped to endure low temperatures. Under lab conditions, I have found that some succumb to freezing at minus 20 degrees Celsius if cooled rapidly, while others can rebound from minus 10 degrees C and crawl about within seconds of being warmed up, like those in the cabin.

The larvae of numerous species of ants and beetles spend the winter inside tree trunks, where they endure temperatures close to that of the ambient air. Unlike the quickly revived flies, the larvae I have brought into the cabin seem stone dead even after hours of relative warmth. Only after a few days do they begin to show signs of life. The substances that fortify these larvae against the cold may also account for their lengthy stupor. Ant and beetle grubs contain glycerol or other sweet-tasting "antifreeze" alcohols (I have not tasted the flies), which prevents ice-crystal formation in the body, renders them inactive, and also takes a long time to leave the blood.

The other winter guests — primarily of three species — are beautiful and benign in habit. When the cabin is heated, for example, they don't have the annoying *P. rudis* tendency to hover around the bed light and then, when it's turned off, to dash under the covers and buzz there rudely.

The first of these, the mourning clock butterflies, usually remain in crevices outside and only rarely make it into the cabin. In the fall I commonly see one or two fluttering under the roof. The second species has arrived here in numbers only in the past few years. These occupy the cabin by the thousands some years and by only dozens in others; this winter, none have appeared so far. They are multicolored Asian ladybugs or ladybird beetles, first introduced to the southern United States to control aphids. Like many of our endemic species of ladybirds, these beetles have handsome red-and-black coloration. Asian ladybugs, however, are more varied. Their "background" hue can be deep red or orange or yellow. They may have no spots or be ornamented by tiny black dots or spots that coalesce into black bands.

Not everyone has fond feelings for these beetles. In some parts of the country, they themselves have become pests due to their sheer numbers as they adapt to life in our dwellings rather than their traditional crevices and caves. And like many other insects whose bright colors serve as a warning to stay clear, multicolored Asian ladybugs taste bad to predators and give off a noxious smell when crushed.

Multicolored ladybugs and their larvae feed on aphids and other plant-sucking insects, such as the woolly adelgid, which is decimating hemlock stands from Virginia to New England. It is claimed that as it develops, a single multicolored Asian ladybug can devour 600 to 1,200 aphids. The adelgid was introduced from Asia and became a serious problem in the mid-1980s, close to the time the Asian ladybird beetles first started showing up in my cabin. Once attacked by adelgids, a hemlock tree dies. So far, I have not had a problem with adelgids on my hemlocks, and I welcome the beetles into their overwintering home.

The third insect that is a regular but never abundant visitor is the green lacewing. The light, bright green of this insect extends to its four wings, delicate membranes stretched between a network of veins. To me, lacewings have a certain aura. But this is lost on aphids. Lacewing adults as well as their larvae, commonly called aphid lions, are ferocious predators. In the woods, I often find the adults hibernating under loose dead bark in the winter. They are rare enough in the cabin to be a treat.

The diversity and abundance of winter wildlife is not unique to my cabin. Anyone can be similarly blessed. By allowing a few openings, I play host to the good, the bad, and the beautiful.*

---

* Since this article was published, both the Asian ladybird beetles and the cluster flies have become rare.

Arctic Bumblebees

Previously published as "The Antifreeze of Bees," *Natural History*, July 1990

FOR THE FIRST TIME IN MY LIFE I WAS LOOKING FOR BUM-blebees at midnight. It was June 22, the second day after the summer solstice. Up here on Ellesmere Island in the Canadian Arctic, the sun circled overhead all day, dipping only to about 10 degrees above the horizon at midnight. But despite the perpetual daylight one would hardly guess that it was summer already. We'd had only four sunny days over the past two weeks of our month here. The rest of the time it was overcast and air temperatures had not risen above 4 degrees Celsius.

Two weeks ago, as we had flown north from Resolute in a Havilland Twin Otter, all the landscape was immaculately white beneath us. As we descended along a steep, bare mountain wall down to Alexandra Fjord, we noticed seals lying next to the holes they chew and maintain through the snow-covered ice all winter long. Polar bear tracks connected some of the holes, and I also noticed with some misgiving that these tracks led up from the shore to the huts that would be the temporary home of our small research party, consisting of Jack Duman and graduate students from Notre Dame University, who had come to study cold-hardiness in insects. I had joined them, hoping to see bumblebees and unlock possible secrets to their thermoregulation physiology.

After the Otter landed on the snow on the fjord and we unloaded our supplies near shore and the plane receded into the distance, we were left in stillness. We crossed ice crevasses on our way to the main hut of this remote Canadian Mounted Police station and there faced a faded picture of a red-coated Mountie blowing a trumpet. There was also a sign, printed in both English and Inuit, next to the gunlock with two loaded rifles, with instructions on defense against polar bears. There was also another sign — this one handwritten, saying, "Enter at your own risk: mad scientists at work." Pick your own risks — inside or out.

We then anxiously awaited spring and the life that comes with it. The lateness in the appearance of tundra life drew our attention to the physical world around us. An iceberg gripped by the fjord ice was below us, and a glacier towered above us to the south. Massive cliffs rose to the east. But I was mesmerized more by the Lilliputian world emerging in small patches at our feet, as the sun started to burn through the snow.

Snow had receded along the gravelly river that was starting to receive the glacial melt. The soil along its banks, richly supplied with granitic pebbles, rocks, and boulders, was covered with a profusion of lichens. There were jet-black, gray, green, white, orange, and yellow lichens, and their forms varied from leaflike lobes, substrate-hugging encrustations, to branched feathery spikes. They grow slowly, imperceptibly, during the brief summers and then they survive in suspended animation during the rest of the year, or most of the time.

Also emerging from the snow were cushions of plants that retain their leaves from the previous year or years. These too are
Methuselahs who survive because they endure the cold, and then
revive again in spring. The low, tight mats of *Dryas integrifolia*
looked like silver-gray rocks from a distance. But in two weeks they
bristled with short greenish-gray leaves, and then they sprouted
their delicate yellow flowers. Branches of one of the numerous
species of creeping Arctic willows had erected catkins looking like
silvery spikes sprouting up from the ground. They soon turned to
red, and then to yellow, before yielding their pollen and nectar to
the arctic bumblebee, *Bombus polaris*.

Saxifraga oppositifolia, the purple saxifrage, the first Arctic flower to bloom, is the first link the bumblebees have to this
physically rugged land. Its small five-petal brilliant purple flowers
shone against the soft and muted pastels of the tundra gradually
emerging from the snow. They opened on smooth green-brown
leaf cushions and perched there, looking as if they might roll off.
To my eye that was not yet accustomed to the biological subtleties
here, or perhaps too accustomed to the physical grandeur, they
seemed precious, especially at first when there were no insects yet
in sight.

However, where there are colorful flowers there are pollinators.
And in half surprise, I finally heard and then saw a bumblebee
zoom near. It was flying fast and straight over the deep snows —
but here, next to me on the very first opened saxifrage flowers,
it stopped briefly and quickly passed on. At this time, it and all
would be females (queens) just now coming out of hibernation,
feeding on nectar to fuel their prodigious energy demands, while
also searching for nest sites in which to found their colonies.

Of the approximately twenty thousand species of bees worldwide, only two occur this far north. Both are bumblebees, and

one is a social parasite of the other. The queens I was seeing now would be those of *Bombus polaris*. The queens of the parasite, *B. hyperboreus*, emerge somewhat later, after its hosts have started their nests.

Above the Arctic Circle, survival for most insects is, as with lichens and flowering plants, largely a matter of slowing down and enduring. For example, as determined by one of my hosts from Notre Dame, Olga Kukal, the caterpillars of the *Gynaephora* moth require about thirteen years to mature. They spend most of their lives solidly frozen, like meat in the freezer, growing only during the brief durations when they thaw out.

Bumblebees are locked into a different life strategy. For them, survival and reproduction depend not on only slowing down in the long winter, but then speeding up greatly during their short window of opportunity. Their larvae (and colonies) cannot survive freezing, and they must squeeze not only their entire growth period, but also their whole colony's life cycle, into one single brief summer season. The "plan" is simple and similar to that of any other social ant, bee, or wasp: a fertile overwintered female strikes off on her own, builds a nest, and lays eggs. Then her first batch or batches of daughters work as babysitters and providers for the later ones, who will mate, overwinter, and lay eggs the next year. The bigger the colony, the better its defense against parasites and predators and the more streamlined the colony efficiency becomes because of the division of labor that is possible.

A bumblebee queen's major limitation to her social strategy is time, because it generally takes the overlapping of several generations of offspring within a single season to build up a colony. This is not a problem in the tropics, where there are few or no seasonal time constraints. Predictably, most colonies of tropical bees, wasps, and ants can become huge. The miracle is that a social insect exists at all above the Arctic Circle.

Arctic bumblebees represent an extreme, and I had speculated about adaptations that might allow them to squeeze a whole colony cycle into a single summer under circumstances that are lethal to other social insects. High body temperature effectively lengthens time, in terms of what and how much can be done, and so how that was done (rather than survival in Arctic torpor at subzero temperatures) was my main focus for finding out here.

Several obvious features help to compress the Arctic bees' life cycle. First, instead of building up a large colony over many generations, the new bumblebee queens and drones are produced after just one batch of workers (and sometimes with no intervening workers). Second, if workers are produced, the first batch commonly consists of twenty or more individuals, as opposed to six to eight in temperate bumblebees. Third, the Arctic bees get a head start by usurping nests already made not only by other bees, but also by unlikely hosts such as snow buntings; I found one *Bombus polaris* queen successfully usurping an active snow buntings' nest containing eggs. The birds yielded to the queen bumblebee, leaving three eggs, and the queen bee then raised her own brood among the cushion of grass and layers of white insulating feathers, leaving the birds' eggs in place.

The major cold-weather adaptations of bumblebees in general, and Arctic bees in particular, however, are their highly developed mechanisms of body temperature regulation, allowing them to be active when many other insects are forced to retire into deep torpor.

Bumblebees can shiver using their flight muscles, heating up to over 35 degrees C above air temperature. As in other hot-blooded

insects, heat is generated in the thorax prior to flight by contracting the up- and down-stroke flight muscles against each other to
produce a tetanus. Like all other bumblebees so far investigated,
Arctic bumblebees require a flight muscle temperature of at least
30 degrees C in order to fly. But flight is slow and clumsy at such
relatively low muscle temperatures, and fast-flying bees heat up
those muscles to at least 35–37 degrees C — nearly the same as our
own body temperature.

For bees, honey buys time, and muscle temperature extends
time; being able to shiver, heat up, and fly are only means to an
end. The gain achieved is an accelerated and steady input of nectar and pollen to the colony. That input allows bumblebee colonies
the time, within one season and on cool days and nights, to grow
even at the prevailing low temperatures because the food affects
foraging speed and the growth rate of the larvae.

In order to grow, the bumblebee grubs must be maintained at
nearly 33 degrees C, which is several degrees warmer than the
temperatures experienced in the lowlands near the equator. And
in order to provide the nearly tropical environment necessary for
the larvae, the Arctic bees and other bumblebees have specific
behavior and physiology relevant to nest temperature regulation.
Physiologically they shiver with their flight muscles and then
shunt the heat produced in the thorax into the abdomen and onto
the brood, much as a brooding bird applies its bared abdomen
onto its eggs and small young. And like a bird on a clutch of eggs,
the bumblebee queen stays pressed upon her brood comb containing eggs and larvae, incubating it so that its temperature stays
above 30 degrees C, even at freezing or subfreezing temperatures.

Like any system that is far removed from entropy, this one costs
much energy to maintain, especially in the Arctic. The purple sax-

ifrage flowers and the willow catkins are all tied together through the energy currency of the nectar from the flowers.

The *Bombus polaris* queens I saw in June skimming over the snow on Ellesmere Island appeared to have little food available so far. I suspected nectar was then more than ever at a premium. Further, I predicted that in order to keep their flight engines heated up, the early-season queens flying in the cold would have to sequester as much heat as possible in the thorax, preventing it from leaking into the abdomen.

My prediction of a low abdominal temperature in the foraging queens turned out to be wrong. Much to my pleasant surprise, I found that the Arctic queens stopping at the saxifrage flowers had *hot* abdomens instead! Furthermore, abdominal temperature was regulated (independent of environmental temperature). Were these peculiarities specific to these northern bees? Apparently so, because back in New England the next spring, comparisons with body temperature measurements of early-flying queens revealed that their abdominal temperatures were lower and unregulated, in contrast to those of the Arctic bees.

Fulfilling predictions is usually not as exciting as refuting them, because predictions are anticipated. I had previously determined in lab experiments that bumblebees' counter-current heat flow to retain heat in the thorax changes to alternating current when these queens heat their clumps of eggs and larvae. The behavior of closely applying the bare surface of the underside of their abdomen to this brood when they incubate their brood is much like a hen heats her eggs. My new exciting hypothesis was this: the Arctic bees were already incubating their eggs in their ovaries, which are of course in the abdomen. Might these bees, having less than one-third the time to build up their colonies than temperate bees do, get a head start on egg development and production by starting to incubate their eggs even before laying them? If so, unlike those of the new queens, the abdominal temperatures of drones and workers would be the same for Arctic and temperate bumblebees — that is, low, because these bees carry no eggs.

Another bumblebee safari was in order. Why not Alaska? This time I came with my friend and colleague F. Daniel Vogt, and we camped at high elevation near Denali. I had again brought my portable electronic thermometer for measuring insect body temperatures.

It was July, when the colonies near the end of the cycle and drones were starting to leave their colonies for their solitary existence of sipping nectar and chasing virgin females. We ascended to about five thousand feet. It was cool and foggy. A sow grizzly and her two cubs ambled below us in a sedge meadow. There were few flowers, and seemingly no bees. The *Dryas* flowers had long since gone to seed. Continuing up the slope, we kept sufficient distance between us and the three grizzlies.

As we got higher we saw occasional bright-blue northern monkshood and larkspur, and a few pale-yellow Arctic poppies. Then, hiking cautiously over a rise where we half expected to see another grizzly, we saw instead a thick patch of arnica, yellow daisylike flowers, blooming in a cool protected wash. Straining our ears above the constant whine of the wind, we heard the drone of a bumblebee, and soon saw many of them. I was elated: they were the fuzzy, heavy-bodied, black-and-dark-yellow-banded *Bombus polaris*. Both drones and workers were working the same flowers, and we started taking the bees' body temperatures. Abdominal temperatures of both were, as predicted, quite low. They were like those of temperate bees at that air temperature.

Abdominal temperature, or any bee temperature for that matter, has little inherent interest for most people. I base that on evidence: While I was professor of entomology at the University of California at Berkeley, the students at Stanford once had a trivia contest to come up with the most trivial thing in the world. The winning entry? "The rectal temperature of the bumblebee." They may have gotten the idea from the *National Enquirer*, where I had been cited for winning Senator William Proxmire's "Golden Fleece Award" for having been awarded $20,000 for studying bumblebees' body temperature regulation, a crucial aspect of bees' lives.

Bumblebees are well-known keystone animals of mountains and the taiga. Like other bees, they pollinate flowers, but unlike all others, they do it also in the Arctic. It is the context that matters, and context is how everything fits together to produce the whole. To see how seemingly arcane details have importance is exciting, because it rings of coherence, and that is the closest thing there is to truth and beauty in this world.

CODA: CURRENT BUMBLEBEE POPULATIONS

Bumblebees have recently been in the news because of drastic population declines in some areas, suggesting possible links to climate change. Because bees are major pollinators in northern regions where they are uniquely adapted to be active because of their ability to regulate their body temperature, one might wonder if weather change has been the cause of their decline. The decline has been highlighted in the public eye mainly by one species, *Bombus affinis*, which in 2016 was put on the endangered species list, a first for any insect in North America. The species was not common, but I knew it well in the 1970s in my study area in Maine. The most abundant species then was *B. terricola*. Bees of this species were so common that I saw dozens at a time in any patch of *Spiraea, Apocynum,* or *Epilobium*. I routinely saw up to several at once on a single meadowsweet or goldenrod inflorescence. Several of my research publications centered on this species because it was easy to get data at almost any time in late summer and early fall. Thirty years later, in the same areas and the same ecological settings, I encounter a single individual of this species only rarely, and some years none. The same situation exists for some of the other species, but so far only *B. affinis* has received endangered species status.

Beating the Heat, and Killing with Heat

Previously published as "Comfort in a Hive: Heads You're
Hot, Tails You're Cold," *Natural History*, August 1993

A FEMALE HONEYBEE WORKER FLYING ON A HOT DAY HAS TO
contend not only with the sun's withering heat but also with her
own internal furnace. To drive her wings, she contracts the powerful flight muscles in her thorax some two hundred times per
second, an exercise that produces a tremendous amount of heat.
The honeybee's internal temperature would reach lethal levels
(118–122 degrees F) and she would "fry" internally in a minute or
two of flight if not for her small size and for the airflow she generates during flight, which dissipates heat by convection. Landing
on a clover blossom to forage on a windless day, however, she also
faces the full brunt of the sun's burning rays. Having filled her
honey crop with nectar and loaded her pollen baskets, the honeybee worker flies straight back to her colony, which is packed with
the pressing bodies of tens of thousands of equally hot hive mates.
Nonetheless, thanks to a few adaptations in their physiology and
behavior, honeybees survive and prosper even in hot deserts.

Most large flying insects have evolved a mechanism to prevent overheating during flight; blood circulating through the flight motor carries heat from the thorax to the abdomen, which gets rid of the heat, much as the coolant circulating through an automobile engine passes through the radiator. The honeybee's peculiar anatomy, however, makes this impossible. The tube that carries the blood from the abdomen into the thorax is thrown into tight coils in the petiole area, the narrow passage that links the two sections of the body. This means that hot blood leaving the thorax must flow around these coils, slowing it enough to heat the cooler blood being pumped into the thorax from the abdomen where little heat is produced — and very little heat escapes into the abdomen. This inability to use the abdomen as a heat radiator might sound like a handicap, but while a radiator may increase the area for cooling, it relies on convection to unload excess heat and would work only if the body is hotter than the surrounding air. Evaporative cooling is therefore the only way any animal can lower body temperature below that of the air around them. Honeybees have evolved such an evaporative cooling system, one that has allowed them to abandon the abdominal heat radiator altogether.

When a foraging honeybee flies at high air temperatures and passive convection no longer suffices to keep her head temperature below 113 degrees F, a thermal sensor there triggers the response to regurgitate nectar from her honey crop onto her tongue. Exposed to the air, water from the nectar on her tongue evaporates, cooling the bee's head and drawing heat away from the adjacent thorax. She can increase the rate of evaporation by "wagging" her tongue and by smearing some of the liquid on the front of her thorax with her legs. A further advantage for bees in relying on evaporation for cooling is that while the forager is cooling herself, she is simultaneously reducing the load of excess water she is carrying and saving energy. By carrying less water, the forager has extra space to transport more calories to the hive, and has also begun the process of converting the nectar to honey (which is concentrated nectar).

On returning, the forager may still be hot, but now she is subjected to the metabolic heat of thousands of her hive mates. The bee quickly passes her nectar to one of the receiver bees that stay within the hive; she then leaves for another trip. If it's hot, these receivers eagerly take up the nectar and cool themselves and the hive by regurgitating it so that it evaporates from their own mouthparts, as well as from droplets they deposit in the honeycombs where the process of making honey continues through further evaporation. As a result, the humidity of the hive shoots up, which stimulates some of the workers to fan the entrances to the hive. This brings in drier air, making continued evaporation possible. If, on the other hand, the weather is cool, few receiver bees will be willing to unload foragers bringing in dilute nectar. Instead, the receiver bees now accept only foragers bringing in concentrated forage. Thus, receiver bees can manipulate the hives' inflow of dilute nectar, concentrated nectar, or water, depending on the temperature.

Bees in the core of the hive or swarm can also become dangerously overheated at modest air temperatures. The outermost bees may be cool, some even approaching their minimum tolerable temperature of 59 degrees F, but as the air temperature outside drops, the temperature at the center of the cluster rises. For many years, researchers assumed that the bees on the outside had some way of communicating with the bees in the core who could, by regulating their own heat output, produce more or less heat as needed. But experiments failed to show any such communication. Further studies revealed instead that the core bees' high temperatures resulted from their resting metabolism alone. But why, then, do the *core* bees get hotter as outside temperatures were lowered? The answer lies with the mantle, or outer bees, who control core temperature.

When honeybees are in a cluster, the outer bees allow their body temperature to "float" passively over a wide range, whereas foraging or otherwise active solitary individuals shiver to maintain a thoracic temperature of about 92 degrees F at all times, making them instantly ready for flight. As their temperature declines, the mantle bees' first line of defense is not more energy expenditure by shivering. Instead, they merely crawl into the inside of the swarm cluster. Increased huddling shrinks the cluster, and air passages to the outside become plugged. Eventually, the outside bees are jammed so closely together that their heads point in and their abdomens stick out. Heat loss of the cluster is then at a minimum, and if the swarm is a large one, the core temperature may shoot to within several degrees of lethal temperatures from the resting metabolism of the tens of thousands of bees crammed together within the swarm, as this heat is trapped within the cluster.

For every action there is a reaction, and overheated core bees do not remain passive. They crawl toward the cooler periphery, thus creating space inside and apertures due to less dense crowding to the outside that let out heat. Normally, both responses occur simultaneously in any one swarm in a dynamic process, and one sees only the net effect as the bees continually shift their position within the hive. Only when the swarm is subjected to sudden temperature changes are the separate actions noticeable. If a swarm is suddenly taken from room temperature to subfreezing temperature, the outside bees feel the temperature change first. They immediately clump, and swarm core temperature shoots up before core bees get a chance to respond. Conversely, when the swarm is suddenly taken from subzero temperature to room temperature, the outside bees lose their cluster, and core temperature plummets.

The power of the mantle bees to affect core temperature is well illustrated by the defensive reaction of the Asian honeybee to predatory hornets. In Japan, the honeybee *Apis cerana* confronts a species of large, heavily armored hornets, *Vespa simillima*, that prey on them. These hornets often patrol in front of an entrance to a weak hive and snatch one bee after another, sometimes depopulating whole hives. Although heavily armed against bee stings, the hornets are not immune to the lethal effects of overheating, which the honeybees have exploited as a defense. At strong hives, the hornets may first be grabbed and held by several bee defenders, and then two hundred to three hundred bees will cluster tightly around the attacker. These defensive bees are already hotter than those just flying off to forage, and as they form a ball around the hornet, they continue to shiver. Temperatures at the core of these small clusters, where the unfortunate hornet is held fast, soar to 115 degrees F. Because the hornet's lethal temperature is slightly lower than the honeybees' (113–116 degrees F versus 118–122 degrees F), the victim at the center of the bee ball dies.

Bee-Lining vs. Bee Homing

BEGINNING WHEN I WAS ELEVEN YEARS OLD IN RURAL WEST-
ern Maine, Floyd Adams, a local farmer, and his family of three
boys, Jimmy, Billy, and Butchie, near my age, introduced me to the
adventure and art of bee-lining. We could not conceive of a greater
excitement than our hunts to find a big "bee tree" full of honey
during late September, when the haying was done and there was
still some wild bloom in the pastures. The bees were then in the
final throes of topping off their honey stores from the remaining
asters and goldenrods.

Our basic tool was a small wooden box with a piece of bee comb
with sugar syrup in it, along with a small sharpened stake with a
piece of board on top to serve as a platform to set the bee box on.
We also brought along a small bottle of anise and some white flour
paste. After finding a patch of goldenrod that was unobstructed by
trees and where we could look in all directions, we stuck the stake
into the ground. Holding the anise-scented bee box in one hand
and a cover for it in the other, we placed the box under a bee on a
flower and slapped the cover onto the box over her. The box was
dark except for light coming through a screen below the honey-

comb, so she directed her escape downward and would bump into and find the syrup, at which point she started lapping and stopped buzzing. We then lifted the cover to see her so preoccupied that she paid no more attention to us, as we placed the box onto the pedestal and then settled down next to it to watch her. In a minute or two the bee crawled up to the edge of the box and rubbed her antennae with her front legs, and we heard her excited hum as she started flying back and forth in front of and all around the bee box, inspecting it closely. Then she started to circle, in ever greater and higher spirals. We squinted to follow her flight, until she eventually disappeared into the distance in the direction where her hive would be. It could be in the nearest copse of woods or several miles away in some distant hollow tree in the depth of deep forest.

We now had to narrow the possibilities of the hive location. Knowing the distance would help for a start, and that could be estimated from the bee's travel time, as we expected her to return for another load of syrup. So we waited. Often in less than ten minutes a bee would suddenly be zigzagging at the edge of our bee box, and then settle down into it to feed.

A bee-line was now started, and soon more bees started coming. We dabbed white flour paste on the thorax or abdomen of some of them to time their flights. If the bee tree was close, our bee box would soon be crowded with bees, coming and going. We then put the cover onto the box to capture many at once, pulled up our stake, and traveled off to set it up again and release our bees at some other clearing or field as close as possible to where we guessed the bee tree might be. When we opened the box, all the released bees flew out, circled around, and most flew off in the same direction as before. This, their first flight at a new location to which they had unknowingly been taken, wasn't much help for us. However, if we were already close to the bee tree and one or a

few bees recognized where they were in home territory, they eventually returned to our bee box. When none did, we captured a new
bee in the vicinity, hoping it might, being closer to its hive, be from
the same colony. Those returning to our box, and resuming their
trips back and forth to their hive, gave us a "cross-line"; the bee
tree would be located at the intersection of the two lines.

We went into the woods to search for our anticipated bee tree
on a sunny wind-still day so we might hear or see the bees in the
air when we inspected one likely old hollow tree after another.
There was no greater thrill than to hear a low hum as we pressed
our ear against an old hemlock (a tree commonly used by the wild
bees) and to see the tiny dark forms streaking above us against
clear sky. Floyd, the usual adult leader of our party, then pulled
his jackknife out of his pocket and carved "FA" into the bark of
the tree. By common convention, no matter whose woods we were
in, the tree, or at least its contents, belonged to the finder. Flush
with the triumph of success, we went home, to dream of bees and
honey. We returned some days later to get to work, after assem-
bling axes, wedges, a crosscut saw, a smoker, gloves, bee veils, and
buckets for the honey and a hive for the bees.

The air was thick with bees the minute the tree fell. They at first
swarmed in a cloud up in the air where their nest entrance had
been. Meanwhile, others were exiting their nest from the fallen
tree. One of us kept busy working the smoker to confuse and dis-
tract the bees, and then with two working the crosscut saw, we
cut into the log above and below where we judged the nest to be
located. Then we drove wedges into the trunk of the hollow tree,
to uncover the bee combs. Those high in the nest tended to be
the newer light-yellow combs, holding the honey. The lower, older
combs were brown, and also contained the brood, the larvae and
pupae. Using a hunting knife, we cut the combs from their at-

tachments inside the hollow trunk, and then lifted them out. The largest, especially those of the brood, we cut to fit into the wooden frames of the hive we had brought. We tied the combs in place with string. (The bees would in the following weeks cement them solidly into the frames with wax, and we would then remove the string that the bees had by then not chewed off.) Honeycombs, if there were many, went into our buckets. When most of the combs had been transferred or removed from the bee tree, we placed our hive onto the opened tree, then gently guided the thickest crowd of bees (which should contain the queen) from inside the tree cavity toward the new hive entrance, with small puffs of smoke.

When the first group of bees had walked as a crowd from the tree into their new home, now reunited with their brood and queen, we could sense their excitement, as they almost suddenly set up a humming. Almost immediately, many bees started stationing themselves at the new hive entrance, where they started fanning with their wings, holding their abdomens up into the air. At the tip of the abdomen they exposed a gland from which they broadcast a scent that in bee language says "Here." The meaning is in the context, and in this context the scent stream they made showed others the way out of the chaos of the lost hive and into a new one that contained their brood. Soon even the bees in the bee cloud up in the air came down, as if by a great migration, as all of the bees relocated. The bees would now begin to cement their combs solidly into the frames, clean up all the honey from broken combs left in the tree, and resume their work of collecting nectar and pollen to shore up their winter stores. Perhaps weeks later we would one evening, after all the bees were home in their hive, plug the entrance and bring it to the farm.

Floyd set a hive in the attic, up against a partially open window. I set up one on a bench of boards behind our barn. It seemed to me like an animal, and I loved to sit next to it, watching it feed itself, seeing paired gobbets of yellow, orange, and white pollen coming in, carried by bees that paid me not the slightest bit of attention. I had seldom been able to see so much from so close.

In the winter I heard a slight humming inside. I reduced the entrance but left an air space for the hive to be able to breathe. Then, in early spring, when there was still snow on the ground, some of the bees finally went out to defecate, each leaving a yellow spot on the snow before returning. But if it was still cold, many that went too far got stranded on the snow and, unable to move from the cold, they died there. Perhaps they were scouts, searching for flowers; it was close to the time when the first pollen would be shed from flowers of the wind-pollinated poplars, birches, beaked hazel, and red and sugar maples.

Pollen is the bees' source of fats and proteins necessary for a colony to reproduce itself through a swarm. It is available mostly in the spring, when the queen can lay a thousand eggs per day, or until the colony has more than doubled and produced another or several new queens. They are then ready to swarm, which involves the splitting of the colony as the old queen and about half of her daughters leave, to eventually find and then settle into a new home in another hollow tree hidden somewhere in the forest.

After the crowd of twenty to thirty thousand bees exits the hive in a big rush, the bees first bivouac in a cluster with their queen, hanging from a branch, looking like a huge beard. Scouts then start to leave, searching for suitable new home sites. With numerous scouts searching, several potentially suitable options may be found. But the swarm must choose just one, and it is usually the best of those available. The queen never leads; she follows the crowd. So how can the vast crowd of tens of thousands come to a consensus, to all end up at the best suitable option for a new home, given that only several of them will ever have seen it before they get there?

At the time I was watching my bees I had, of course, no idea. Nor did I even conceive such a question. What biologists had already discovered then I could not even imagine. But I did get a glimpse of mystery. And perhaps due to our bee-lining, and my preoccupation with the hive of bees in the back of the barn, my father gave me a present. It was a thin book of giant proportions. It described experiments by a biologist, Karl von Frisch, in Austria. Each of his experiments demonstrated a specific fact of bee behavior. And fact upon other fact from more experiments connected together to make a story of sheer beauty, the elucidation of the bee language.

The experiments of von Frisch were something like our bee-lining, but much more systematic. The bee-lining revealed how bees that we had fed with syrup in the field had apparently communicated with their hive mates in the hollow of the hemlock tree, so that they would come to our bee box, expecting syrup, even though they had never been there before. But von Frisch's systematic, and yet not more complicated, experiments cracked the code of *how* they communicated. Martin Lindauer, a student of von Frisch, went on to make other systematic observations showing how scout bees in a swarm of tens of thousands search for nest sites, and after finding one report its direction, distance, and their estimate of its suitability back to the swarm. With multiple scouts reporting multiple possible home sites (which in the case of Lindauer's endeavors were mostly cavities in bombed-out ruins in his hometown — this was right after World War II) back to the stationary swarm, there is huge scope for confusion. But Lindauer nailed the bees' solution to the problem so well that he was able to go and meet the swarm at its intended goal, because he had read the messages of the bees and knew which site the swarm would fly to before it had even left.

As mentioned, the scouts may find a half dozen or more available potential homes of varying worth, and each one is advertised by a scout to the swarm (just as the bee that found our bee box advertised it to its hive mates). This involves the scout bee communicating direction and distance from the hive through a dance language. Bees follow the dances and accurately interpret the information given as to direction, distance, and worth, and then fly to the source and check it out. They may, on return, follow another dancer and check out her find as well. Then, based on a comparison, the bees advertise *the best of those tested;* when what another has found is better than what they know of, they readily convert. When all agree, a signal is given and the swarm leaves to settle into the best option for a home. However, the story does not end there. Bees that know where the destination is become "streakers" — they zip fast through the aerial throng in the correct direction.

I felt fortunate, on a sabbatical leave from the University of California at Berkeley (where I had worked out the mechanism of swarm temperature regulation), to be at Harvard and residing in an office by mere chance with Thomas Seeley, then a PhD graduate student. He has now spent an illustrious career at Cornell University, continuing the work on honeybees, which von Frisch likened to a magic well: the more you take, the more there is in it.

Seeley has worked out the increasingly fascinating details of how, from their home inspections, the scouts evaluate the relevant real estate in terms of bees' worth, and how a swarm socially coordinates itself to manage the transition from its parent hive to the quarters it has chosen. He had also engaged in the sport of bee-lining, starting it after reading a piece I had written about introducing bee-lining to my then-young nephew Charlie Sewall.

It was published with our photographs in 1975 in the *National Geographic School Bulletin.*

Forty-one years later, bee-lining in the forests around Ithaca, New York, led Seeley to another unanticipated and quite important discovery.

Honeybees were in trouble from disease die-offs mainly due to industrial agriculture, with its correspondingly industrial beekeeping for crop pollination. Honeybees were becoming increasingly endangered by rampant mortality, and the only remedy in sight was increasing medications. However, Seeley found that in

This sketch shows honeybees fanning while stationed at the nest entrance. They may be fanning to cool the hive or also dispensing pheromone that guides others to and into the hive entrance.

the forests near Ithaca, where unmedicated bees presumably also died, there was nevertheless a thriving wild population. There is always genetic variation in a natural population, and the likely explanation was that bees with resistance were evolving by natural selection, so that the forest has indirectly produced a resistant strain. It was another example of the value of forests, found indirectly by following a thread of nature for the love of the adventure in doing so.

Seeley has now written a delightful book about bee-lining, one that I suspect will someday become to some girl or boy what von Frisch's book was to me. According to the French philosopher of science Henri Poincaré, "The scientist does not study nature because it is useful; he studies it because he delights in it. And he delights in it because it is beautiful." This delight is in our nature, and felt acutely in childhood.

Beetles and Blooms

Previously published as "Bedouins, Blooms, and Beetles,"
Natural History, May 1994

THE ASSOCIATION OF INSECTS AND FLOWERS SCARCELY
attracted attention for centuries. It was simply a given, and the
idea of bees being intimately connected with plant reproduction
would have seemed absurd. Finally, in 1793 a schoolteacher in Germany, Christian Konrad Sprengel, pieced together in a book (*Das
entdeckte Geheimnis der Natur im Bau und in der Befruchtung der
Blumen — The Discovered Secret of Nature in the Construction and
Fertilization of Flowers*) a scenario proposing that flowers are the
reproductive organs of plants, where fertilization occurs through
the agency of bees, and where the flowers have signaling devices
and food rewards to attract the pollinators. People had of course
seen bees on flowers for millions of years, but they had not been
aware of what they were seeing.

Sprengel's view of sex in flowers must have been breathtak-
ing for him, but his idea was dismissed as a "fairy tale." Flowers
providing food to attract bees, and having signals to guide them?

Indeed! His biggest critic was the polymath Johann Wolfgang von Goethe, who said that to consider Sprengel's idea to be true meant assuming that Nature operated by and according to a *human* logic. Since Goethe was the preeminent German thinker, writer, and scientist of his time, the criticism implying that Sprengel had a fairy-tale mentality had an unfortunate sting: Sprengel was fired from his teaching job at Spandau, accused of *Pflichtvergessenheit* (neglect of duty).

At that time there was still no inkling of the concept of evolution, much less coevolution. Nobody could know that any single biological fact has potentially two very different (but both potentially correct) explanations: the immediately proximal causation and the ultimate (evolutionary) one. The latter may look like purpose or intent, which tends to be considered a uniquely human capacity — hence, Sprengel's problem. His ideas, referring to the result of an ultimate evolutionary causation, were presumed to point to human intent, and therefore they were summarily dismissed. His thesis drifted into obscurity. A century later, however, when Charles Darwin read Sprengel's book in the light of evolution, he saw its significance. Since then, Sprengel's "discovered secret of nature" has afforded a view of our planet so grand that I suspect even he would have been skeptical of its huge implications. They reach from the level of plants and pollinators to the composition and functioning of whole ecosystems.

This idea, which was being explored in the 1970s, included more than my previous work on bumblebees and flowers. I learned, for example, that individual bumblebees of any one species learned to become specialist foragers on the flowers of specific but different plant species. They thereby increased their foraging profits by learned skills in flower finding and handling, as they carried pollen from an individual plant of one species to another flower of the same species, rather than indiscriminately among plant species, which would not promote cross-pollination. In a natural habitat historically populated by the same species of plants, those plants in turn co-evolved to accentuate flower differences that favored the bees' becoming specialists (and hence reliable pollinators of those plants).

When the growing season is short, plants are constrained to flower within a narrow window of time, placing a selective pressure on them to diverge in flower morphology. Yet each attribute can be and usually is a product of many selective pressures, and each of different value, so that the balance of the evolutionary result at any one time and place can shift from one to another product specific to that time and place. Given this perspective of community ecology, I was surprised that at least in early spring, various species of northern spring woodland flowers growing under closed forest canopy, such as anemones, for example, were white or light-colored. Was that because they were shaded by the forest and white was a more conspicuous target for a bee from a distance?

In my correspondence with the Israeli biologist Avishai Shmida, I then learned that in the Judaean Desert there is similarly a strong convergence of a diversity of plants that have flowers of one model — in this case, large red flowers. Red is associated as a strong signal to hummingbirds, and many tropical plants that they pollinate have red flowers, but in the Judaean Desert there are no hummingbirds.

An unusual pattern is always interesting. I thought I had long since finished involvement with pollination. But Avi told me that my 1972 *Science* paper on pollination energetics was required reading in one of his courses at the University of Jerusalem, and that "it has stimulated us to look at our flora in a new way." And he invited me to visit him and see flowers there. Not only that, he procured funds to cover my expenses. My duties, he told me, were to "do exactly as you like!" I came gladly, spurred by the prospect of seeing the red bloom of desert plants and their insect pollinators. I had to go!

As the plane landed in Tel Aviv, I looked over the crowds of strangers — and could not find my friend Avi. Finally, after an hour, he arrived. He had been stuck in a traffic jam in Jerusalem, where the former prime minister Menachem Begin had just been buried.

On our way to Jerusalem, we stopped at ancient terraces cut into the hillsides where wine was made in Roman times; in pits scratched out of the limestone, workers had trampled on grapes to squeeze the juice from them. Along mountain roads I saw scattered almond trees in flower, with brilliant white and pink blossoms. Purple cyclamen, red poppies, and blue grape hyacinths grew wild.

We passed the remains of an ancient Roman road, built of steps cut into the solid rock. The top of each step slanted up, cut that way so that chariot wheels would not roll down the hill. In the third and fourth centuries the road was used to haul chalk from mines in Beit Guvrin to plaster houses in Jerusalem. The chalk pits are now huge underground caves inhabited by hundreds of jackdaws — small pretty crows with a gray nape, black face, and white eyes. They flew in and out of a hole in the ground leading to these ancient pits. They had colonized the chalk caverns since about 1950. Before that they had come only in the winter as migrants from Europe. Now, with plenty of food available at a nearby dairy kibbutz, they stay year-round rather than return north to Europe.

Nearby, at Netiv HaLamed-Heh, is a large hill, which like the nesting cavern of the jackdaws is also of human origin. It's a "tell," the remains of a settlement of 3000–500 BCE, which is now a mound covered with bright-blue patches of blooming lupines, *Lupinus pilosus*, mixed with groups of purple-pink cyclamen like that commonly sold in garden stores back home. Bright-yellow daisylike composites were scattered throughout, along with Carmel orchids, *Ophrys carmeli*, plants that deceive bees by offering them flowers that look like female bees. These orchids are also scented like female bees, inducing the males to try to mate with them and thus pollinate the orchid. (Of course flowers are the sexual organs of plants. It seemed ironic for one to be providing sex for an animal.) I inserted a twig into one of their flowers, and when I withdrew it, it carried a yellow pocket of pollen, such as a promiscuous male bee might transfer to the next *Ophrys* it visits. Avi showed me another orchid whose numerous tiny flowers resembled a colony of aphids. Syrphid flies whose larvae feed on aphids lay their eggs here, and thereby pollinate the flowers in the process. This long-overgrazed country has been occupied for thousands of years, yet has 2,387 species of wild plants supporting an estimated 1,500 to 2,000 species of bees (only 800 had been recorded to date). How many other stories of pollination might there be?

The Judaean Desert in the spring was, as promised, mostly a sea of red bloom, within which were scattered the red crown anemones, *Anemone coronaria*. Their flowers, when young, have dark centers. Their crimson red color was intense. Each flower has male and female components, with the female stage preceding that of the male by two or three days; self-pollination is avoided because the pollen (male part) is shed only after about ten days after fertilization has taken place. When pollinated, the flower

signals this state with a white ring. Each flower releases a mean
of two million pollen grains, which are suited for wind dispersal
to close flowers and by insect dispersal to more distant neighbors.

In a vacant lot near my apartment in Jerusalem many crown
anemones (of the family Ranunculaceae) were in full bloom,
and they had small scarab beetles on them. Most flower scarabs
eat pollen, and may fly swiftly between flowers, yet these beetles
seemed sedentary. In many I saw pairs in copula. Did the flowers
serve not only as overnighting spots but also as trysting places for
the beetles? The sexes must meet somewhere, so why not while
lounging at conspicuous, well-advertised places where there is
pollen, needed by the females for laying up protein stores to make
eggs? Indeed, I observed male beetles landing on flowers containing a beetle, and instantly attempted to mate with it.

Food rewards were apparently of only secondary concern for
the males. I surveyed 1,548 flowers in this lot and determined that
if one flower held a beetle, then it was thirty-five times more at-
tractive to other (male) beetles than an unoccupied flower; the
flowers almost literally put out the "red carpet" to attract beetles.
Although the females were proximally attracted by the pollen, the
main animal pollination could have been the male beetles hunting for them. The females stayed in place while the males kept
moving from flower to flower until a female was found. It is an
apparently winning combination; in southern Africa in the Na-
maqualand desert, another scarab–flower association involves a
daisy, *Gorteria diffusa*, that has ornamental petal markings that
mimic beetles closely enough to fool people into thinking they are
seeing real beetles.

Here it was not only the crown anemone that had red flowers.
Daisylike flowers that in Maine are white or yellow were represented here by the red *Adonis* (family Compositae). The desert

poppy (*Papaver asiaticus*, family Papaveraceae) was red, and while buttercups (Ranunculaceae) back home are bright yellow, those here (*Ranunculus asiaticus*) were red, and looked superficially like the local poppies and anemones.

About fifteen species of plants in the Mediterranean region of Israel evolved to have large, red, bowl-shaped flowers. The convergence is most striking when one considers how some of these flowers differ from their likely ancestors. *Ranunculus*, the buttercup, for example, has about four hundred species worldwide. Only three are red and all three occur only in the Mediterranean region. All of these have cup-shaped flowers at least twice as broad as those of the predominantly yellow or white species elsewhere. Wild tulips in Europe are also predominantly yellow, but in the Mediterranean region, they are mostly red.

That red, bowl-shaped pollen flowers evolve in so many different kinds of plants in one geographical area is distinctive. From behavioral studies of bees, one could speculate that once a pollinator becomes "hooked" on one commodity — such as red flowers — it could then be more easily exploited by other plants, provided they are rare or bloom slightly out of phase with their models. Avi had documented that although there is overlap in flowering in different species, peak flowerings of the species are indeed separated, as one species' bloom follows another's through the short season. This sequence is not due to random chance, because if one of the species of the ecological guild is missing in a certain area, then the other species flowering either just before it or after it extends its flowering period to fill in the otherwise empty time slot left by the missing species.

These red flowers are rarely pollinated by bees. Instead, when not wind-pollinated they are primarily serviced by scarab beetles of the genus *Amphicoma*. As Amots Dafni, of the University of

Haifa, and six colleagues from other institutions reported in 1990, these beetles have a weak response to shape or scent, but have a strong attraction to the color red. Dafni and colleagues distributed unscented, flower-shaped plastic cups of various colors (red, blue, yellow, green, brown, white) in the field to serve as beetle traps. Of the 146 beetles captured in these cups, 127 were caught in the red flower models. The 18 remaining beetles were evenly distributed among the other colors. These are the same beetles I had seen often in the red anemones. But they are found too in all of the red flowers of the poppy guild. Pollen is a reliable food for those beetles, and they are behaviorally evolved to find and use it, but red flowers probably have more to offer these beetles than pollen. Red color also advertises sex to them, and after the beetles use that color as a signal in an early-blooming species, later-blooming ones in turn "use" the beetles conditioned to the same color signal. Thus, a specific selective pressure can swamp others.

The flowers, in their critical flowering times in the desert, are advertising overnight shelter with sex and breakfast in bed — a winning combination. The *Amphicoma* beetles in the Judaean Desert get the red carpet treatment, and we enjoy the show.

Cooperative Undertaking: Teaming with Mites

Natural History, May 2017

THE UNIVERSITY OF GUELPH ENTOMOLOGIST STEPHEN A. Marshall, a recognized authority on flies, has described how green- and blue-bottle blowflies (family Calliphoridae) deposit their eggs "almost before the body hits the ground." And they oviposit their eggs in batches of 150–200, up to 2,000 each. In summer heat, these eggs hatch in hours and develop into flies within days. Sarcophagid flies, or flesh flies, may sometimes get a jump-start on blowflies with live births of their larvae. I have counted up to ninety-five blowflies arriving at the carcasses of porcupines, raccoons, and woodchucks within minutes. At 30–32 degrees Celsius, their maggots reduced these carcasses to piles of skin, bones, and hair in three days.

In summer, carrion is a hotly contested resource. Numerous species of insects vie with one another and with some mammals and birds to get to a fresh carcass and consume it before competitors can. In Maine, blowflies usually finish first and dominate other competitors at larger carcasses. With smaller carcasses of species such as mice, shrews, and songbirds, however, burying beetles, also called sexton beetles, of the genus *Nicrophorus* (order Coleoptera, family Silphidae), often arrive and quickly move the goal — that is, they carry away a carcass and bury it, to be consumed later, underground.

Large mammals have the strength and size to easily move carcasses by themselves. But for a nicrophorid beetle to move a bird or mammal carcass — weighing up to two hundred times its own weight — and then bury it, cooperation between mates, mites, and even potential competitors is involved.

One summer evening, I noticed a species of sexton beetle common in Maine, *Nicrophorus tomentosus*. It was perched stock-still on stilted legs on a pine stump. The tip of its abdomen was stuck up in the air, with the membranes of its pheromone-producing glands conspicuously exposed. The beetle was, presumably, broadcasting an alluring scent to attract a mate. I waited. Soon, a beetle of the same species came zigzagging back and forth, flying close to the ground. In color, size, and flight pattern it was almost indistinguishable from a yellow fuzzy bumblebee; if I had not seen a study of this beetle's mimicry, I would have presumed it was one of several species of the yellow-and-black bumblebees.

Male and female *Nicrophorus* beetles are nearly identical in size and markings. The one that came flying in was, no doubt, following the scent trail of the perched beetle. It quickly narrowed in on the stump and landed. The seemingly comatose beetle then suddenly ran to the new arrival, climbed on its back, and mated. Mating of beetles and other insects typically involves prolonged periods of "mate-guarding," during which the male remains attached to the female for hours and perhaps days, thereby precluding or reducing possible sperm contributions from rivals. But here there was no mate-guarding; the couple separated within several

At left: Nicrophorus tomentosus *beetles, mimicking bumblebees in flight.*

seconds, and the newcomer — the one I had presumed to be male (given the usual insect behavioral protocol) — flew off. The previously motionless one resumed its rigid pose, with abdomen tip up in the air, presumably wafting pheromones.

I was disoriented on two points. First, sexton beetles are among the very few insects in which pairs form and cooperate in raising their young, using the food (the carcass) that the pair has stored underground, where they settle as a couple. But these two showed no signs of bonding. Second, also according to usual insect protocol, the pheromone-calling is done by the female to attract a male, but in this case the sex roles were reversed. Or had I seen incorrectly? To find out, I remained to watch for further developments. In just fifteen minutes, another beetle of the same species came flying in, and the previous behavior was repeated almost exactly.

Intrigued and disbelieving, I waited still longer, and within an hour the same pattern occurred a third time.

As I learned later, I had not been mistaken. Male *Nicrophorus* beetles were known to broadcast scent to attract females, although the reasons are unknown. After realizing the need for speed in carcass-carrying and burying, I suspected that for these beetles, the usually prolonged mating protocol had been suspended, as an adaptation for securing food. The beetles needed to get ahead of the flies before they colonized the food supply with maggots, and perhaps at a carcass about to be taken by them, courting behavior might be a distraction from the priority of carcass burial.

Other apparent anomalies abounded. In contrast to the apparently mated pairs usually observed at mouse carcasses, I found that, of the dozen or more *large* carcasses that I examined (from porcupine up to deer and moose), not one was attended by pairs of beetles. In summer, the bulk of these carcasses went mainly to maggots. On the other hand, chicken-sized carcasses were either taken over by maggots with no nicrophorid beetles, or they were populated by one or two dozen beetles at the same time. Sexton beetles were apparently attracting one another to the same bait by broadcasting pheromone. I saw up to nine *Nicrophorus tomentosus* beetles arrive one after another at one mouse carcass, where several beetles with their hind ends up were releasing pheromones, while another deer-mouse carcass close by had none. Clearly, more was going on than a mated pair feeding their nest of offspring. From observations, I suspected that the answer involved mites.

Most sexton beetles arriving at carcasses are covered with dozens of yellowish mites. Many species of mites suck blood (I've seen them kill entire broods of baby phoebes in their nests). Yet nicrophorid beetles make no attempt to scrape off the relatively large and conspicuous mites, nor defend against them. They are tolerant because the behavior of *these* mites works to the advantage of the beetles, since the mites feed on fly eggs.

After a beetle lands on a carcass, mites jump off to seek fly eggs and young maggots to feed on from the crevices between hairs and feathers. They use beetles to transport them to their food. With numerous beetles offloading mites at the same carcass, the beetles inadvertently help one another preserve the carcass from becoming fly-blown. Mites, however, may not be essential if a pair of beetles buries a small carcass quickly; but for larger carcasses, mites buy the couple time, and that edge is essential.

Although many beetles participated in the early stage of food processing, later, some beetles started to leave, and after a carcass was buried, usually only a pair remained. The pair used the carcass as a nest to rear their offspring on and in. They removed its hair (or feathers) and applied saliva onto or into the carcass. The beetles' saliva contains compounds that deter or kill bacteria, the second most important competitors for their food.

One of the more puzzling aspects of the beetles' cooperation was not the processing or ownership of a carcass, but the moving of it to a suitable burial place. How do beetles physically transport a carcass, and how do they collectively pick a destination so that they do not work against one another by moving in opposite directions?

In one experiment, I put out five just-caught deer mice (genus *Peromyscus*) in an area of several square meters. No beetles took to them the first day, but on the following day each mouse had one or more *Nicrophorus tomentosus* beetles attending it. To test which, if any, of the mice they might transport, and how far and how, I placed two of the mice on twenty-centimeter-square shingles of bark placed on moist, loosened soil. Beetles removed the mice from the hard, flat surfaces and buried them in the soft soil nearby. I placed the other three mice on hard, dry ground strewn with fine loamy dry soil, which should have been easy to dig in but was not deep enough to bury a mouse. Within an hour, beetles had moved these mice ten centimeters along the dry sandy soil to suitable burying spots with loose loamy soil. An hour later, after dark, two of the mice were buried, with only their tail ends protruding from the ground, while the remaining mouse was only partially buried. The beetle attending it was sometimes under it and then would wander off for a half meter or more. It would return and wander off again but in a different direction. It dug itself under the loose chaff and soil, then emerged, and wandered some more. Its behavior seemed haphazard, but perhaps this was a clue — the beetles apparently search for a suitable site before they start to move the host carcass.

The next morning the mouse belonging to the wandering beetle was no longer visible. Not even the tip of its long tail was sticking out of the ground. I dug all around looking for it; it had been moved. I then dug where the beetle had wandered several times, and there, at eighty-three centimeters from the original spot, I found the buried mouse, but it now had a pair of beetles under it. Either one, or the pair, had transported the mouse, an animal at least a hundred times heavier than either beetle.

The beetles never visibly pushed or pulled the mouse carcass, but slowly moved it (the pair were out of my sight, under it). To find out what they might be doing required an experiment. I took a window screen and hoisted it between two stumps so I could lie under it and look up after placing a patch of suitable soil for a mouse burial at one end of the screen, along with the carcass of a short-tailed shrew and two attending beetles. Lying on my back below, I watched the pair of beetles move the shrew carcass across the window screen to the pile of earth. The smaller beetle of the pair did most of the scouting, and the other most of the carcass moving. Each beetle crawled under the carcass and, with its back planted to the screen and facing the opposite direction of the soil, grasped the shrew tightly with its legs and walked it forward with its legs, while the beetle itself stayed in place. When the beetle reached the other end of the shrew, it emerged, righted itself, and walked back to the other end of the shrew. Both beetles repeated this maneuver until the pair had moved the shrew to its burial place. There, they pushed the soil from under the carcass to the sides, so that it sank into the soil.

After a carcass burial, a *Nicrophorus* pair spends weeks out of view in their underground lair, raising their brood. They feed the young a slurry of partially digested meat before they feed on the carcass themselves. The male then leaves, with the female following some days later, each to repeat the cycle of finding a mate and a mouse.

Nicrophorus tomentosus *beetle pair cooperatively moving a short-tailed shrew carcass to a burial place, while blue- and green-bottle flies get ready to start laying eggs on it.*

I have sometimes seen *Nicrophorus tomentosus* perched on leaves and grass stems, though more often in flight. Unlike most nicrophorid beetles that fly by night (probably for safety), this species is diurnal. Being able to occupy the day-carcass-hunting niche, it may gain an edge in finding and claiming carcasses before night-flyers get going. A special feature makes that possible.

All *Nicrophorus* species are black, and most have bright-orange bands across their elytra (wing covers). These striking markings are impossible to miss. But the moment a *Nicrophorus tomentosus* beetle takes its first wing beat, one sees bright yellow instead. As already mentioned, the beetle looks like a bumblebee, acts like a foraging bumblebee, and sounds like one. The magic of sudden bumblebee mimicry is striking, and scientific papers have described it, featuring the yellow color as derived from the yellow fuzz on the thorax. That yellow is indeed conspicuous and it is part of the display, but the sudden disappearance of the bright orange bands on black was not mentioned. This seemed odd, since the wing covers of nicrophorids of this and other species remain folded over the abdomen. The yellow seen in flying beetles has apparently been attributed only to the thorax. Yellow was certainly conspicuous, but why the sudden absence of orange, and the absence of mentioning the absence? I would have dismissed it also, if I hadn't watched the beetles' behaviors and then also looked at their anatomy.

Sexton beetles depart from other beetles in their flight mechanism; in some, the elytra are spread laterally during flight, like the wings of an airplane. In others, they remain closed over the abdomen as a shield and also to reduce air resistance and ensure fast flight, as in some scarab beetles. In the sextons too, the wing covers shield the abdomen in flight, but the normally orange-and-black surface of the wing cover is twisted and totally flipped, so what was down before flight is suddenly up. The hidden yellow and fuzzy elytral undersurface is now in full view. This makeover to the appearance of a flying bumblebee occurs in a fraction of a second at the initiation of flight. The beetle is now protected from bird predation because birds do not catch bumblebees; their sting is too painful. This mimicry, therefore, allows this species to fly freely in daylight, presumably unlike beetles that lack this feature. Discoveries cannot be looked for; they happen like this one, mostly by rummaging around in semi-familiar territory.

Whirligig Beetles: Quick Paddlers

Natural History, December 2017–January 2018

SKIMMING OVER LARGE BODIES OF WATER IS A FAVORITE
pastime all over North America. Whirligig beetles (family Gyrini-
dae) have been doing it for at least 200 million years, from at least
the beginning of the Jurassic period. If threatened, they may dive
and stay underwater, breathing oxygen from an air bubble held
on their back, under their wing covers. As it is used up, the oxygen
in the bubble is replenished by partially extruding it to the water
(where the bubble acts like a physical gill; oxygen from the water
diffuses in, and carbon dioxide from the respiration of the beetle
diffuses out). The beetles may also fly to another pond, lake, or
stream if the one they are on or in becomes unsuitable. Usually,
though, these shiny black beetles, up to a centimeter in length, idle
conspicuously on the water's surface. I found thousands of them
in the late 1970s on Lake Itasca in northern Minnesota, where I
helped teach a field course at the University of Minnesota's Field
Station located at the edge of the lake.

Along the shore of Lake Itasca, I saw these whirligigs aggregated into tight groups, or pods. Hundreds and sometimes tens of thousands of individuals occupied a square meter. They barely moved except when I paddled within several meters of them, at which point they made the surface boil with their frantic swimming; then, within ten to fifteen seconds, they reaggregated and settled down in the same place. *What could these beetles possibly be doing, loitering all day in large flotillas?* I wondered. Yet after dark, the individual beetles' V-shaped wave tracks were conspicuous as they skimmed along near shore, far from any pod. I wondered where the isolated beetles had come from, and where were they speeding to. I thought the question might be answered by chasing the beetles by canoe, and because canoe skills would be essential for following these fast skimmers, I recruited Dr. F. Daniel Vogt, then a biology student and an athletic outdoorsman, to help.

Over the next three weeks the beetles put our canoeing skills to the test, as Dan and I almost daily and sometimes nightly canoed a survey course along the twenty-two-kilometer shoreline. We found twenty-seven beetle pods, totaling approximately 400,000 beetles. Each pod contained from 50 to an estimated 200,000 beetles. Day after day each pod remained in its same place, but the number of beetles in some increased, while those in others decreased. Yet we seldom saw a beetle singly during our daily excursions in sunshine along the idyllic shores, where the dragonflies gamboled among nodding wild rice and waving bulrushes. On the other hand, we routinely saw individuals in the dead of night and during cold dawns. Contrary to what had been supposed, we found that the beetles were nocturnal.

The beetles started to move about twenty minutes after sunset, when the water surface around a pod became roiled. Periods when the beetles were milling about alternated with times when they stayed quiescent. As it got darker the pods expanded, and beetles, alone or in small trains, started to leave the pod vicinity and travel in straight lines along the shoreline. Those that approached our canoe grabbed mosquitoes that we swatted and dropped down to them; thus, they were apparently out on their scavenging hunts. They were not likely finding prey only by sight (although their eyes are double, with one part underwater and the other above it), but by a different mechanism, using their antennae.

The antennae of most insects are long and sometimes also plumose, and are used primarily as scent detectors. The whirligigs' antennae are short — barely visible to our naked eye. They are instead adapted as a sonar device, for detecting obstacles and prey.

The base section of each antenna rides on the water surface (while a short club-shaped portion is raised into the air just above the water surface). The antennae have mechanoreceptors that stimulate a nerve at the respective antennal base, when the respective right, left, or both antennae are lifted due to a disturbance of the water floating the antennae. The beetle's brain decodes the incoming mechanical information from the antennae, in terms of the direction and nature of the water disturbance (Friedrich Eggers, 1927). The way the beetles hunt for food — by bursts of swimming, which we saw among beetles at night — creates pulses of waves that then inform the beetle about the nature and behavior of an object immediately ahead of it by the waves that are reflected from it. (The same principle of animal sonar was discovered in 1940 by Donald Griffin, who proved that bats locate flying insects in the dark by pulsing sound waves and detecting the echoes reflected from them.)

Those beetles in the vicinity of their pods zigzagged or moved in small circles, making rapid movements but achieving little if any net forward motion. Those leaving their pod traveled in fairly straight lines at about thirty meters per minute (about fifty body lengths per second), fast enough to potentially move 0.8 kilometers (the average distance between rafts) in thirteen minutes.

At any point over a hundred meters from a pod, net beetle traffic was away from it in the early part of the night, in both directions at midnight, and primarily back toward it before dawn. Perhaps some beetles "homed" to the rafts of their origin each dawn, as this data suggested. To find out, we had to identify some beetles with respect to their pod of origin, so we captured and marked 680 beetles from one large pod.

Our capture strategy was simple: We positioned our canoe about a hundred meters from our targeted pod, with one of us standing poised in the bow of the canoe, holding an insect net. The other, in the stern, paddled as vigorously as possible directly toward, into, and through the raft. The catcher with the net made several quick swipes through the pod before the beetles had time to disperse or dive. We then daubed our beetles with red paint on their elytra and immediately released them to rejoin their pod, as it came back to rest.

That night, as usual, numerous beetles left their pods to travel up and down the shoreline of the lake. Within two days, we had resurveyed all our previously located pods. Marked beetles had reappeared not only in their original pod, but also in nearly all of the pods in the two large arms of the lake. This showed that the beetles were capable of joining pods *without* homing. Subsequent observations of beetles in the vicinity of pods also provided clues as to how the beetles may aggregate to produce the relatively permanent pods, even without homing. The mechanism involves following one another, as we found by following them.

Many of the beetles remained at or near their pods all night, foraging in the vicinity of the pod by zigzagging about individually. Near dawn, however, the beetles started following one another. They produced trains of several arranged one behind another, which joined up with still others. The more beetles in a group, the slower its net rate of movement, as one beetle swirled around another. The more they followed in the crowd, the less net progress was made in moving elsewhere. Thus, swarms of beetles contracted into the original pod cluster, the nucleus of which was defined by those that had stayed.

Whirligig beetles feed only at the water surface, where they scavenge and capture prey caught in the surface tension. Their ability to find food depends on close encounters because their sonar system works only within several centimeters. Speed of travel translates to distance traveled, and to the number of prey encounters per unit of time. Therefore, the beetles' water-skimming speed has likely been under intense selective pressure, accounting for their highly streamlined and smoothly tapered form. Their oily covering likely also minimizes drag.

The beetles' first pair of legs serves as a tong specialized for grasping, while the last two pairs are adapted as paddles. The middle pair rows at twenty-five to thirty times per second and serves also in maneuvering. But the last pair is the beetles' main analogy to a boat propeller, churning the water at fifty to sixty beats per second (twice as fast as a dragonfly beats its wings).

Waves are a large part of a whirligig beetle's world, and wave mechanics are important to it, as they are to a boat's performance. Objects on the water surface create two kinds of waves. One, called capillary waves, are those pushed up at the bow. The other, gravity waves, are those left in the stern of the moving object (or vice versa). The bow wave provides a barrier, and hence resistance to speed, and ships take advantage of that phenomenon for energy economy by adjusting their speed accordingly. Similarly, for maximum speed and lowest energy expenditure, whirligig beetles swim not *over* the waves, but in the trough between a capillary wave in the front and a gravity wave behind.

Although the beetles' morphology and physiology explain many aspects of their capabilities, including *how* they can hunt at night, they did not reveal to us *why* they were nocturnal on Lake Itasca, nor why they aggregated into pods. However, other features, and comparative biology, did give hints of likely explanations.

A beetle skimming along on the water surface is easy to locate because the wave it leaves behind on each side of it on the water is visible from afar. A moving beetle could therefore be an easy target; a fish hunting by sight would find it almost impossible to miss. But if the fish recognizes a beetle by its wake, as a bird recognizes the red color of a ladybird beetle, it would learn to avoid the obnoxious taste of its foul-smelling defensive secretion (gyrinidol, a sesquiterpenoid aldehyde). Some ladybird beetles also gather into huge aggregations. They may be highly visible due to their aposematic coloration (color that serves as a warning), but they are also protected by foul-smelling secretions.

An aggregation of gyrinid beetles should be a safe place for each individual. Not only does it dilute the individual's risk of attack, but also it pools their noxiousness, enhancing the defense: the bass or sunfish living in the pod area would soon become familiar with their sight and taste, and would avoid them. However, fish in the middle of a large lake, far removed from a pod there, might perceive the beetles' waves as a strong stimulus for attack. To test whether such fish are potentially attracted, we ferried beetles out to the center of the lake and released them. As predicted, fish rose to catch them there, but we did not see any beetle get taken that we released at or near one of their pods. The beetles' aggregations and nocturnal foraging therefore likely relate to a defensive strategy against fish predation.

RAVENS AND OTHER BIRDS

Ravens on My Mind

Audubon, March 1986

SNOWFLAKES LAZILY SPIRAL EARTHWARD, CATCHING ON THE browned brittle heads of goldenrod, field spiraea, and fireweed. Only recently these plant skeletons had sported yellow, white, and purple flowers that stood out against the green grass. Bumblebees had scrambled over the flowers, frenziedly competing with each other for tiny droplets of nectar and pollen. This pollen and nectar had provided food to produce new queens, now underground, being gently covered by layers of cottony, insulating snow.

The woods are silent. The white-throated sparrow, ovenbird, and hermit thrush have flown south. Field and forest are left now for only the winter-hardy: chickadee, blue jay, coyote — and the northern raven, *Corvus corax*.

On this day, as on innumerable others this winter, my mind is on ravens as I peer across the snowy field through a crack between the logs of my unfinished cabin. A hundred yards in front of me, down by the edge of the woods, is their bait — two calf carcasses. Sitting for days on end in an unheated cabin, watching for a bird to come by and feed, is not exciting — unless one is fired by a burning question. I am. Do ravens, possibly the most intelligent of all birds, cooperate with each other in finding food? That question grew from an earlier puzzling observation, one that might have been predicted by socially foraging bees instead, like the wild honeybees we had lined here as boys, but not in solitarily nesting ravens.

Like many other field observations, this one came as a pleasant surprise. I had been taking a casual walk on a cool crisp morning. Recently fallen leaves were tinted with frost, and my footsteps crunched deep into them. I heard blue jays calling from the ridge above. A flock of evening grosbeaks flew over the beech trees, whose trunks were scarred by bear claw marks.

All was as I had remembered from countless other Maine autumns. Except now, in the distance, I heard ravens. But there was not just one, or two. And their calls were not just the usual *quork, quork* one hears on occasion as two birds fly over, keeping voice contact with each other. These calls sounded like high-pitched yells, like those the young make in anticipation of food, when a parent comes to feed them. There was excitement in these calls, and they kept coming from the same place about a half mile away. I didn't need plainer language to understand that these ravens were calling because something had stirred them. Following their calls, I discovered it was a moose carcass, or the remains of one. A bear had torn into it, and most of it was covered in brush, but the flesh was still fresh. The coyotes had not yet arrived. And in the meantime, more than twenty ravens were having a feast.

You can hardly miss a raven in these woods in winter, but I had not seen any for days. One bird could have found the carcass by chance perhaps. But twenty? My credulity did not stretch that far; I had to have a better answer. Even if twenty birds had found this carcass independently, that would not mean they would voluntarily share the feast. One would expect instead that it would make sense for ravens relying on carrion during the winter to fight over a carcass, because it is vital to their survival.

On the other hand, cooperation is common in the animal world, and it is often the key to survival in hostile environments. It is not difficult to envision how a strategy of cooperative foraging in ravens could be to their advantage. If twenty independently foraging ravens somehow communicated and shared each food bonanza they discovered, then any one raven would have nearly twenty times greater a chance of having more food on a regular basis, despite perhaps having less of a massive amount of food at once. In winter there is little else to feed upon except carcasses. And since they are rare, each one is cleaned up within several days by mammalian predators and scavengers. Thus, by sharing a carcass the ravens may not be giving up much, if anything — because the greatest part of any kill is a temporary resource that is consumed by large mammalian carnivores. To test the validity of this theory of cooperation I set out animal carcasses throughout the winter. A deer, a goat, or a calf would presumably be consumed almost overnight after a pack of coyotes had found it, but several ravens' feeding could leave hardly a noticeable dent.

Superficially the woods near my camp in Maine look no different now than they did twenty or thirty years ago. At that time I already knew them well. On the light snow in November, the white-tail bucks wandered in search of does, and I trailed them through the beech-maple forests, down into the fir-cedar swamps, back up again through the hardwoods, and up onto the spruce-clad ridges. There were no tracks of major predators — no wolves, no coyotes, no cougars. And I seldom heard or saw a raven.

But things have changed in twenty years: coyotes and ravens

have moved in, nearly simultaneously. From camp I often hear coyotes howling at night. I daily see their tracks in the snow, and after about ten hours in the woods I often see a raven or at least hear one in the distance.

There is much speculation about why coyotes arrived and settled here. The prevalent view is that they came from the northwest, filling a niche left when the wolves were wiped out. But why did the ravens come at about the same time? Was it because of some kind of association between the two?

I satisfied myself that no ravens would have been feeding on that moose carcass were it not for the predators that had ripped it open. Ravens have strong beaks, but they are unable to take more than the eyes and part of the tongue of an undamaged moose's head. Neither were they able to penetrate the hides of deer, goats, calves, or raccoons. Indeed, carcasses that were not ripped open by predators were left virtually untouched by the ravens. Often a raven or two would come by for a brief daily visit, as if checking out whether or not feeding could begin.

The ravens' association with some predators is well known. Ravens follow wolf packs, and they have been reported to be attracted even to the howls wolves make after a kill. The Inuit claim ravens follow polar bears, apparently waiting for them to make kills. Because of the close relationship of ravens with predators, it seemed conceivable that these birds could discover a dead animal, perhaps one that had died from starvation, and then make noise to call in a scavenger, maybe a coyote. The ravens rely on the predators to make a kill, or on scavengers to dig out animals that have died and become buried in deep snow. However, in my experiments all of the ravens that discovered whole carcasses remained silent. None tried to attract a scavenger. Clearly, the calling at the moose carcass was not meant to alert coyotes or bears.

Ravens have an immense repertoire of calls, and no lexicon of their sounds exists. However, one of their common family of calls at a rich food source, the "yelling," is similar to the "place-indicating call" described by the German scientist Eberhard Gwinner, who has studied captive ravens. He had observed the place-indicating call in fledgling young, who apparently use it to indicate their whereabouts to parents, and in the female at the nest. If the birds cooperate in food finding, then it seems appropriate that they would also use this call, or yell, at a rich food bonanza.

There is no doubt that the calls can be a powerful attractant: I recorded the yelling the ravens made at an opened deer carcass and played it back in the absence of food. On several occasions ravens flew directly overhead. Clearly, if the ravens had wanted to minimize sharing the kill, they could have merely kept silent. To be sure, there were occasional squabbles at a carcass where many ravens were congregated, but of greater significance than the squabbles was the fact that dozens of ravens routinely fed at a single carcass at the same time.

Cramped and cold, watching in my cabin since dawn, I now find my scientific curiosity tested. I'm eager to see just one of the sleek shiny birds, to hear the swish of its wing beats. It might be hours, or days, before one arrives. But one will arrive, sometime. It always does. But after it does, how will it behave, and when will the others come?

Sometimes no raven appears for two days. But today one flew over at 9:40 a.m. It circled back and stayed in the vicinity of the clearing for twenty-four minutes, yelling its place-indicating call and making the usual raven *quorks*. Then it left. But three hours later it or another returned with a second raven, and the yelling resumed. There was silence for an hour, but then ravens called again. By late afternoon I saw four simultaneously.

None of the ravens descended to the bait. But then one made a strange knocking noise that sounded like a metallic drum roll. The drumming sound continued at intervals of several minutes, and then a raven approached on foot out of the nearby woods. It got almost up to one of the calves, then flew back nervously as if afraid, only to return in a few seconds for another approach. The bird seemed to be frightened, yet hungry. A strange bait, like these calf carcasses, could easily hide a trap that has been set for coyotes. Do the ravens know of this danger from previous experience? The raven retreated. None touched the calves this day.

When I resumed my vigil the next dawn, a raven was already calling in the nearby woods, and more could be heard yelling at intervals throughout the morning. Occasionally one swooped over the bait. More ravens came, after long intervals when none seemed

Common ravens — acrobats in the air.

to be in the vicinity. Near noon there were suddenly six of them. Four descended simultaneously, formed a phalanx, and advanced cautiously side by side on foot toward the closer carcass. With outstretched necks, they continued to advance, until one pecked at the calf. Instantly they all jumped up and took flight. But within fifteen seconds the four regrouped and repeated the same maneuver, only this time five others swooped in and joined them.

It seemed that all of the ravens wanted to feed, but none dared to be the first. Then nine advanced together on a broad front. Again the group took flight after one of them pecked at the calf, and again they regrouped for another advance. After several such tries in short succession, they finally stayed and began to feed, and by late afternoon at least twelve birds were coming and leaving independently.

The snow, which was sporadic, then started developing into a

storm, and by the next morning the calves were buried. Unless the
birds could shovel snow, their feast would be brief.

Five inches accumulated during the night, but the ravens
came shortly after dawn. Six of them perched on the snow-covered branches of spruces. They preened their fluffed feathers, and
made soft croaking sounds. Others called from the nearby forest.
They flew repeatedly over the site where the calves lay buried, and
one landed there, briefly jumping up and down nervously before
leaving. By six o'clock they had all left. When no more ravens could
be seen, I left the cabin with my tape deck and loudspeaker, hid
under some spruce branches, and played the raven "yelling" that
I had recorded earlier. In four out of six trials one or two ravens
appeared overhead within fifteen seconds. I had never seen a more
beautiful sight than those ravens. Of course this had worked before already, but the implications are too important not to do it
again, and again. To me it seemed like a miracle each time. They
recruit, and share!

Coyotes came the next night; I had heard them howl the previous evening from a neighboring ridge. Their story was written in
the snow. They came as a group, and in two days there was nothing left of the calves. Where might the ravens feed next? In these
woods that I have walked for many winters without finding more
than one carcass, I did not envy them their task.

When I finally lit the evening fire in my cabin stove that night,
I already felt warmed inside from seeing that the ravens' sharing
behavior of food is indeed real, and that it is more important than
I had originally supposed. It resulted in the availability of food to
each individual, and also may have decreased the perceived risk
that any individual might face when feeding at an unfamiliar bait.

I think now of honeybees, which are more likely to land where
others are already feeding, and which recruit at short range by

broadcasting scent rather than sound. But how did the ravens recruit others from such long distances? Is there a raven "dance" that incites or invites followers at a communal roost? What was the function of the drumlike calls? The raven, who cocks its head at me as it flies by along the ridge, now holds more secrets than before.

Coda

The preceding observations set the stage for my continuing study of the ravens' apparent sharing and their many other behaviors. The sharing was real. But after successfully capturing the birds and marking them for identification as individuals, I found that their sharing was probably based on selfish motivation. Ravens are not altruists. They do what they do because there is something in it for them. Similarly, I recruited numerous helpers for my raven study who expended considerable effort because it was rewarding to them as well.

A Birdbrain Nevermore

Natural History, October 1993

THE ANCIENT VIKINGS REVERED RAVENS AS MESSENGERS OF the gods, and Native Americans of the Pacific Northwest gave the ravens the role of benefactor in their mythology. Even today, in Ireland, a wise person is said to have "raven's knowledge." How has the raven acquired this reputation? Is the bird truly intelligent? Just what do we mean by animal intelligence, and how can we measure it or distinguish it from instinct or from learned behavior?

The underlying assumption of intelligent behavior is not performance but consciousness, something nearly impossible to test directly. Nevertheless, animal consciousness has increasingly become an object of scientific inquiry. Donald R. Griffin, a professor of zoology at Rockefeller University of New York and Harvard University, defined consciousness in terms of intentions. "An intention involves mental images of future events in which the intender pictures himself as a participant and makes a choice as to which image he will try to bring to reality . . . The presence of mental images, and their use by an animal to regulate its behavior, provide a pragmatic, working definition of consciousness."

One of the first scientists to attempt to show that animals other than humans have such conscious insight was Wolfgang Köhler, who in 1917 reported on some then-extraordinary observations of chimpanzees. Köhler had placed a banana out of reach of six hungry chimps in a room that contained a wooden crate. Most of the chimps eagerly jumped up, trying to grab the banana. One of them, however, held back, then pushed the crate under the banana, climbed on top, and grasped the fruit. Was this a lucky coincidence, instinct, learning, or a demonstration of insight? In 1984, researchers at Harvard University gave pigeons a variation of the banana test. Like the chimpanzees, the birds could push a perch to reach food, but they first had to be *taught* to move the perch and also to hop onto it. No pigeon spontaneously "got the idea" without prior learning; none had the insight to perform correctly what had not been first demonstrated overtly.

Insight in birds had been posited at least fifty years earlier by a number of researchers who described caged birds such as finches and tits pulling on strings to draw food toward them. However, the behavior could have developed gradually by learning instead. The few critical studies of this behavior showed slow learning instead, but no sudden leap of performance, as might be supposed if the bird had a sudden mental flash of the problem and its solution.

What I'm leading up to, of course, is ravens. Many people would like to believe that such magnificent birds are intelligent, and I thus here state my bias. I love ravens and their relatives the crows. But my appreciation of them is not altered one whit by whether their behavior is guided by insight, learning, evolutionary programming, or by some combination of these that surely applies in varying mixes to different behaviors in different animals, including ourselves.

Whatever its origin, ravens' behavior is remarkable. That said, I will also venture to comment that published proof of the raven's intelligence is nonexistent. The raven's braininess was, so far, not a matter of fact, any more than were its fabled cunning, divining powers, mischievousness, and sense of humor, although all these were accepted as truths for centuries. What has passed for raven intelligence can conceivably be explained by other hypotheses.

I have applied this conservative approach to numerous reports of raven intelligence. A note in a recent ornithological journal, for example, describes a pair of ravens throwing rocks at two researchers who had climbed to the ravens' nest on a desert cliff. The distraught raven parents remained directly above the interlopers, dislodging stones that dropped onto them. So far, so good. But was this a calculated response to a threat? It may have been, but a simpler explanation may suffice. Whenever I have climbed up to ravens' nests in Maine and Vermont, one or both of the parents usually stayed and displayed their anger by landing close to me, all the while violently hacking at anything near them. Since these were tree nests, the birds, unlike the cliff-side ravens, had a number of perches available to them. They perched on trees near but not directly above me, and the twigs they tore at fell to the ground instead of on me. Thus, the action of the rock-throwing ravens could have been basically the same as that of the frantic tree-nesting ravens. Context could make the rock-raining behavior on the cliff appear to be intelligent, and that in the forest irrational.

A second published report describes a raven jumping up and down on a lawn where voles had tunneled beneath the snow. The author concluded that the jumping was a deliberate attempt to flush out the voles. Yet I have observed hundreds of ravens perform such jumping jacks whenever they are nervous near potential food. They do it off snow as well as on, and next to a dead raccoon as well as next to any strange object, and sometimes merely if they are skittish. Perhaps it is an evolved reflexive response that allows the birds to elicit reactions and distinguish live from dead bodies.

Another class of often-reported "evidence" for raven intelligence involves birds working in teams to achieve a common rational goal. In the usual scenario, a predator (such as a wolf, fox, or eagle) holds food that a pair of ravens want. One raven will perhaps sneak up behind the feeding predator and peck or bite it on the tail, and when the predator turns around to face its assailant, the second raven rushes in to grab the food. This happens routinely, and has often been cited as an example of foresight and intelligence. But ravens (and crows) will also harass dogs and other predators (but not a companion) in the same way when no food is in sight. My pet crow has amused me many times by its habit of biting the tail of my neighbor's dog. And my tame ravens similarly approach and nip strange and potentially threatening objects or animals. If several ravens discover an eagle eating a fish, they will loiter nearby, waiting for an opening. One of the birds might tweak the predator's tail for any of a number of reasons. Another bird then simply seizes the opportunity to grab a meal. No conscious foresight needs to be presumed to account for the superb cooperation. Insight, such as seeing an opportunity, is certainly not excluded, but conscious cooperation is not demonstrated.

Some behaviors, however, defy easy explanations. When feeding on suet, ravens, crows, blue jays, woodpeckers, chickadees, and nuthatches usually hack or tear off bite-sized portions in a feed-as-you-peck strategy. Near my home in Vermont, a pair of ravens often came to feed at suet, but remained nervous in the presence of humans and tried to minimize the amount of time spent near the house. One day I inadvertently flushed one of the members of the pair from a large, frozen chunk of suet. Instead of pecking at the lump and extricating bits of the fat, this bird had chiseled a groove three inches long and more than a half inch wide. Scraps of fat were adhering to the groove, so that if the bird's objective had been to eat only at the moment, it could have done so easily, then and there. Yet by gouging out a sizable portion, the raven (had I not flushed it) could have removed and carried off a much larger piece of suet than it could have eaten piecemeal in the same amount of time. It appeared to have sacrificed immediate gratification, and expended a considerable effort at the time, for harvesting a greater reward to use later. The raven's suet carving appeared to be a vivid inscription of a raven's plan of comparing the immediate to the potential later reward, and seeing the steps to achieve it. But it was not proof.

I devised an experiment to test for the role that conscious insight might play in behavior. I needed to present the animals with a simple task that required many separate steps. In addition, no reward could be given for partial completion of a task, so that learning one step at a time would be eliminated. (Such an approach contrasts strongly with the usual learning paradigm, in which a researcher or trainer conditions an animal to complete a task by gradually shaping its behavior through rewards.)

My first subjects were hand-reared American crows. I housed them in an outdoor aviary abutting a picture window of my house. In addition to a long, horizontal pole for perching, the cage contained small trees. I gave these tame crows a simple mechanical problem that involved pulling a string to manipulate a piece of meat from a distance. Since they were hand-reared aviary birds, I knew they had never seen or used string. I suspended the meat from their horizontal perch by a string some twenty-five inches long. Most but not all children (as I found out by questioning them) can easily visualize a solution: to obtain the meat, a bird would have to land on the perch above it, reach down with its bill, pull up a loop of string, step onto the string to anchor it, release the bill, reach down again to pull up another loop, and so on, in a repeating cycle of more than twenty steps, until the meat was raised to the perch. All of the steps have to be executed in a precise sequence. Because each of the mechanical steps is extraordinarily simple, the whole task itself is simple — but only if a creature has insight. The problem is more complicated for a bird that has no concept of the string's connection to the food or what it can do to exploit the string to the food. I doubted that a bird could solve the problem without a lengthy, tedious learning process.

When I left the dangling meat, both of my crows (which I had not fed in a day so they would be suitably hungry) immediately showed an avid interest in the food. They examined the hunk of meat, flew at it, then pecked and pulled at the string where it was attached to the perch — exactly as young kids told me they would do if they were a bird. But the meat on the string was ignored within fifteen minutes. After that first day, I continued to watch the crows from a picture window, to be absolutely sure I didn't miss anything. I finally stopped watching but left the meat hanging, changing it on subsequent days and offering all sorts of delectable food on strings. Thirty days later the bait was still hanging. The crows had failed to figure out how to gain access to the meat, and after that they ignored it. I am confident that I could have easily taught them, had I started with a short enough string so they could have reached the meat with just one pull. However, there was no point for me to even try. I was interested in what they "knew," and I was confident they might learn, just as I knew that bees know how to make and store honey because they are programmed that way by instinct.

The crows were interested in the meat; as soon as I lifted it up for them and placed it on the perch, they invariably grabbed it and tried to fly off with it. Each time they did so, the meat was yanked out of their bills before they had flown two feet. They did not comprehend that it was attached to something. However, after five and nine such trials, respectively, the two birds refused to fly off with the meat, and instead ate it in place on top of the perch. If they were induced to take flight, they then always dropped the meat first. This showed that they could quickly learn to avoid having the food wrenched away, but they still did not draw the conclusion that they could pull the meat up by using the string. These results were precisely what I had, with my cautious biases, expected.

I subsequently gave the same test to five tame ravens, housing them in the same outdoor aviary where I had housed the crows. The ravens also immediately closely examined the dangling meat, but I had the impression that they retained an interest in it even though they were not instantly able or willing to reach it. Unlike the crows, they kept glancing at it, as though studying the situation. After about six hours one raven landed on the perch, reached down to pull up a loop of string, stepped on it, reached down again, and completed the whole sequence of pull-step-release-pull to reach the meat. I was amazed; I knew the bird could not have "practiced" because I had been watching the ravens without pause for six hours. This bird had performed the sequence flawlessly on its first attempt. I then immediately chased the bird away from the perch before it had a chance to eat the meat it had acquired. When it took wing, it spontaneously dropped the meat. Within seconds it was back, again eagerly pulling the meat up with the string. Now it could not be kept away. Every time I chased it, it dropped the meat before lifting off. Its string-pulling behavior had not been a fluke.

Given what I knew about the background of this captive bird, these behaviors were objective proof that the bird "knew" how to get the meat. Furthermore, it confirmed that it knew enough to drop the meat *without* any trials or practice.

Three more of the five tame ravens (all marked with conspicuous numbered tags on the wings) followed suit, showing sudden proficiency in the string-pulling task. While these three birds could have learned from the first raven, I doubt that this was the case, since the first raven's performance was by a direct "pull-up" technique to hold the string at the same spot, whereas two of the other ravens instead used a "side-step" to pull the string along the perch. Learning through observation would not preclude insight on the part of these birds, yet the crucial maneuver — pressing and holding the string to the perch by the toes by *applying the appropriate pressure* — was invisible. Like the first raven, none of these ever attempted to fly off with meat they had pulled up.

In science one rigorously applies the simplest hypothesis first. If that does not fit the facts, then the next most logical is tested. The simplest explanation of these results was that the ravens had behaved with respect to this problem by referring to a mental process similar to ours, with insight into what they were doing in terms of mental images that provided connections. If they had not employed that capacity, then the outcome would indeed be extremely puzzling. I wanted to try to disprove that they "knew." To do that I first needed to try to trick them.

Did the successful ravens now automatically associate string with food, and would they pull up *any* string, without examining whether or not meat was actually attached? I hung two strings, an inch or two apart, from the perch. One held a piece of meat and the other a stone of equal weight. Without insight but from learning that pulling up string produces the desired food in sight to appear, I expected both to be pulled up with nearly equal frequency. But in over one hundred trials, the ravens *never once* pulled up the rock. In their haste, however, the ravens often *contacted* the wrong string by pecking it or giving it a brief tug. These mistakes were precisely the ones I now found most useful in delving into the basis of the birds' behavior. One tug was generally enough to let a raven decide whether or not to *continue* the entire sequence of steps, and I had the distinct impression that the ravens looked down as if to watch the meat. If they saw the meat move, they knew they had the right string. If the rock moved, they jumped back immediately to correct their mistake.

After they learned to look even before they tugged, I was able to test more specifically what they looked for and what they saw. I *crossed* the two strings, fixing them in place with fine thread. Two of the ravens *consistently* first tugged on the wrong string (but nevertheless still always pulled up the right one). Their consistency of choice amazed me. They made the *same mistake* twenty times in a row, as if not only unable to learn but also unable to try the other string. In other words, learning the facts was necessary to *overcome* an insight — in this case, one based on a wrong insight. Their behavior was not random. Despite being dead wrong, they were apparently convinced they were right. The other two birds made *no* mistakes on the crossed-string experiment, right from the beginning. Thus, the same overt behavior was based on two different internal thoughts: "pull on the string over the food" or "pull on the string connected to the food."

The ravens, so far, had experience only with sisal twine. However, the way to access meat was not to pull on sisal twine as such. It was instead to pull on whatever happened to be connecting the food to the perch. Had the ravens gotten this essential point, or had they merely made an association between *sisal twine and food*? When I presented them with a choice of green woven string holding meat, and sisal twine attached to a stone, they pulled only the green woven string, which they had never seen before: they knew the *essential* point without ever having learned it by trial and error.

I then hung up a sheep's head on which the ravens had already been feasting, and near it a small piece of meat on another string. *I* knew that they would be unable to hoist the heavy sheep's head, much less hold the string holding it up in place with one foot or even both feet. But would the ravens know this also, without learning by trial and error? Was their previous success due to a series of mere arbitrary mechanical steps, which miraculously resulted in the appearance of food? As before, the ravens surprised me. Not once did they try to pull up the sheep's head.

My five sets of observations and experiments make highly plausible the idea that some ravens can form a mental image of at least one problem and its solution. Learning occurred, but the observations absolutely cannot be explained by shochorning them into the notion that the behaviors occurred in the absence of insight. While insight can follow learning (at least, most of us who teach dearly hope so), the results with ravens show that it can also precede learning.

I later gave the same test to two groups of wild-caught ravens, of fourteen and thirteen individuals, respectively, in a huge outdoor aviary in Maine. After just fourteen minutes, one bird deftly pulled up the meat. But finally, only three birds in one group and four in the other "knew" how to attain the prize. This gap in performance argues against this behavior being instinctual, and also perhaps against observational learning. Sometimes the exceptions prove the rule.

CODA

In this case the exception may have been the scientific publications of this study showing insight. As a graduate student I had published in the international journal *Animal Behaviour* how *Manduca sexta* sphinx moth caterpillars reach and consume a leaf that is far out of reach of their feet, without moving from their perch. My point was that a seemingly purposive behavior is explained by using two strictly instinctive mechanical rules. My manuscript was immediately accepted for publication.

The ravens' behavior in accessing food suspended on the string involved insight, and the manuscript showing the data of the experiments was also submitted to the same journal (in July 1991). After five successive and seemingly excessively long-delayed responses, it was rejected by the same and two other animal behavior journals to which it was sent subsequently, on the grounds that it did not supply an "objective definition" of insight that the data could be referred to for fit. I indeed did not provide an objective definition of insight because I knew of no objective means to define what goes on in the mind. I felt instead that the results of the experiments were perhaps the first objective definition of what insight means. The paper was finally accepted in 1995 by *The Auk*, a bird journal.

Ravens and the Inaccessible

Orion, Autumn 1995

IT IS HARD TO GET TO KNOW A WILD CREATURE, ESPECIALLY so for a scientist, who must be unbiased and cannot presume that a wild creature is somehow like a human, despite knowing a human is an animal. For as Henry Beston once said about animals, "They are not brethren, they are not underlings; they are other nations, caught with ourselves in the net of life and time, fellow prisoners of the splendor and travail of the earth."

For twelve years I have been trying to illuminate the "nations" of the so-called common raven, *Corvus corax*. I'd like to see the world as through their eyes, as I must before I can understand them. Thus, I have to go into their country. Even here they are shy, because for many generations they have been driven to shun humans. Accused of killing lambs, they were poisoned at baits. They were shot for "sport," as "varmints." In New England ravens were nearly driven to extinction. Those few that remained nested in remote mountain crags far from human intrusion.

Now, happily, they are edging ever closer to human contact

because, since the collapse of sheep farming, they are no longer persecuted as presumed vicious lamb killers. The most recent nest I found was in a pine tree, in back of the parking lot at a car dealership in Farmington, Maine.

I saw my first nest about thirty years ago. It was (and still is, every year) in a tall white pine near a small, isolated mountain lake, the home of a pair of loons. I had been walking on the crusty snow in March, along the leatherleaf-bordered frozen lake, when I saw two large black birds with wedge-shaped tails. Their resonant rasping calls confirmed that I was near a nest, and I soon saw it in the crown of one of the larger pines. The snow beneath the tree was littered with freshly snapped-off aspen twigs that had fallen from the nest platform. Both birds circled at some distance from me, but as they banked I saw the sun flashing off their burnished wings, which glinted like polished metal. Their calls varied from deep, long, angry-sounding, rasping caws, to series of short, high, flute-like calls, to xylophone-like staccato sounds. I had no idea what any of them meant, and for the most part, I still don't.

The tantalizing wonders of the birds' home life were so remote, so inaccessible, that they exercised my imagination. My romance with the otherness of corvids had been instigated by a pet crow I had as a child. It was now rekindled, and would become a consuming passion. Years later at a moose carcass surrounded by a crowd of exuberant ravens, I began to wonder if, how, and why ravens share huge food bonanzas. To try to answer those questions I've raised young ravens from babies and lived with them. With friends I've dragged stillborn calves, expired cows, and road-killed deer and moose deep into the snowy Maine woods. With John Marzluff and other friends and colleagues, we've captured, marked, and released 463 ravens to plot their movements, interactions, and identities. Some answers are now available and secured in technical journals.

But to really know the wild raven, I wanted to see its home life up close — to observe it raising its young. I would not get my first look into a raven's nest until after many years of studying them from a distance. By chance I found a nest on a cliff with a view from the top of an adjoining cliff. Woodland grew to the edge of the cliff, and at this edge I built a hiding place by laying spruce and fir branches over a hole dug into the deep snow. It was late February. Through a peephole in my blind I had an unobstructed view down into the nest, about thirty feet away. In order not to disturb the ravens I did not again venture near my pygmy hut until the young had hatched, in late April. As before, the alarm sounded when I came, and when the birds left I crept into my blind. I was prepared to wait.

Barry Lopez has written, "If you want to know more about the raven, bury yourself in the desert so that you have a commanding view of the high basalt cliffs where he lives. Let only your eyes protrude. Do not blink . . ." I knew from previous experience that this statement was only partially true — one cannot allow even one eye to be within range of their sharp eyesight. The raven is cautious. I flattened myself against the far wall of my cave, and hardly blinked. Hours may have passed. But it was a warm spring day and the first wave of wood warblers had returned — the yellow-rumped, the black and white, the northern waterthrush, and the ovenbird. The very air seemed suffused with birdsong. The yodeling of the red-winged blackbirds was almost drowned out by a chorus of wood frogs, which in turn was periodically interrupted by a bittern's resounding booms — *ka-thunk, ka-thunk* — and a Wilson snipe's whinnying challenge. A winter wren searched for gnats in my thicket of twigs, and then erupted in a vibrant refrain, while an eastern phoebe called from a dry branch near the cliff below. But the ravens, both adults and young, remained silent. I peeked down at the four pink youngsters growing a black stubble of pinfeathers. Their limp bodies lay heaped into a pile. Occasionally they squirmed weakly in their deep nest cup of fluffy deer hair. They slept.

I was shocked out of my reverie by the sharp ripping sounds of powerful wing beats reverberating from the cliff walls, as if off a drumhead. A raven landed on the thick, dry twigs of the nest's edge. Instantly four heads shot out of the nest mold, and their bright-red open mouths waved back and forth like tulips in a breeze, to the accompaniment of loud begging calls. In less than a second the big bird inserted its bill into one of the gaping maws and promptly regurgitated meat from its crop. The youngster swallowed greedily, now making sounds faintly like a churning motor. Then it wilted down into the nest as the parent fed the next one.

One youngster backed up to, but not quite over, the nest edge to try to relieve itself over the nest rim. It succeeded in the first, but not in the second. The adult gently picked off the white fecal sac and swallowed it. It then inspected the nest closely, picking out other recyclables. Then the raven launched itself down to an aspen tree just below. Its mate took its place at the nest, and also left quickly. The domestic chores done for the moment, the couple then briefly sat side by side basking in the sun, making soft cooing sounds. She (for I could now compare them) nuzzled up to him and bent her head down, and he responded to her solicitation by preening her feathers on the back of her neck, as requested.

This experience reverberates in my mind, each detail of behavior like a dab of color in a great painting of the birds' world. Each dab of color is nothing when in isolation, but the whole makes each a beautiful picture. I felt the privilege that comes with seeing what many others have not seen. And I pondered what I might have felt had I seen "it" instead on the television screen by pressing a button and watching it along with millions of other viewers, and whether or not I'd have been moved to experience this day as I had. I wondered how much we had gained by instant gratification, and how much we had lost.

There is value in the inaccessible. Maybe inaccessibility is a value. And the raven is a part of the wildness and unknown regions that Thoreau wrote about. He said that we sometimes need to wade "in marshes where the bitterns and the meadow-hen lurk, and hear the booming of the snipe [sic], to smell the whispering sedge where only some wilder and more solitary fowl builds her nest . . ." The most uncharted marshes, the most inaccessible wilderness, and hence to me the most seductive aspect of the raven, is not only the place where it dwells but also its mind, which is an adaptation to its unique life. What whispering thoughts are at the edge of the raven's mind? To seek answers is like looking for windows to another planet, or to see ours from another perspective.

I may have learned much about the raven after these twelve years. For instance, I have learned that it shares out of self-interest, and I now know some of the mechanics of how and why the crowds assemble from afar at a rare food bonanza. I have an inkling as to what a few of its calls mean. However, I have also learned that its mind, like the immortal wilderness, is not fully accessible to our experience. We can, with sufficient effort, be rewarded by elucidating puzzles or by peering into its nest to see its home life. But secrets are never divulged easily, nor should they be.

A common raven, Corvus corax, *in neutral posture when at rest.*

Space exploration ain't easy, either, but knowing the difficulties, you appreciate it all the more. Perhaps it is better to make trails to the edge of the wilderness rather than through it.

If you venture to the edges of things, you reach out to try to see mysterious vistas, for it is the far reaches beyond the horizon that attract. That is why ravens, like other creatures, will be forever fascinating. They invigorate and appeal to the wonder that is the basis of our humanity.

Phoebe Diary

Natural History, May 2000

ALMOST TWO HUNDRED YEARS AGO, JOHN JAMES AUDUBON attached a silver thread to the legs of a pair of eastern phoebes nesting in a cave on his father's estate in Pennsylvania. This early American experiment in bird banding paid off: Audubon was delighted to see the birds he had marked return the next year. A few of these insect-catching songbirds may still nest in caves; others build their nests under cliff overhangs. But today, like barn swallows and adaptable imports such as house sparrows and rock doves, many eastern phoebes raise their young near humans and their structures: under bridges, in barns, or beneath the eaves of houses.

My first intimate contact with these dark-to-smoky-gray birds with the white bibs was in 1951, when my family moved to Maine. A pair nested in our three-seat outhouse. Later I nailed a small piece of board onto the underside of a beam in the barn. Phoebes built there the next spring, and they continue to do so today. Probably most farmsteads close to woods in the Northeast and the

Midwest host a pair of phoebes. For five months of the year when I lived in rural Vermont, my family and I enjoyed watching a near-tame mated pair raise two successive broods of four to five young. Phoebes help mark my annual cycle, one that begins, come spring, with their arrival back "home" from their wintering grounds in the southern United States.

My diary for March 24, 1998, records that year's first intimations of the phoebe's return. A warm wind that day was rapidly melting the remaining snow. Down in the bog, the first red-winged blackbirds were yodeling, and a robin sang in the evening. I went to sleep hearing the wind.

I awoke suddenly in the night, almost sure I had heard a phoebe. But I could see only darkness through the skylight above my bed. I went back to sleep thinking this would be a great night to migrate. If I were a phoebe, I might ride home on the wind.

The next night, from the maple tree just outside the bedroom window, I heard it again, a phoebe's excited *dchirzeep, dchirzeep* call. There was just the faintest glow of dawn in the sky, and I jumped out of bed to look. Perched barely five feet from the window, the phoebe wagged its tail up and down (a characteristic move), stretched a wing, and continued calling. I made a cup of coffee, took notes, and waited for dawn.

Daylight revealed two birds. Phoebes typically refurbish an old nest or build a new one on top of the old. This pair wasted no time inspecting the two spots where they had nested in previous years. One was the bend in the drainpipe by the bedroom window, the other a one-inch ledge just above the back door. Each time one of the pair landed on one of the old nest sites, it made a soft chittering call and vibrated its wings. Quickly the pair decided on the back-door site.

The male's dependable greeting starts the day, every day, for two months. The "song" can be described as a short, high buzz-whistle or can be likened to the sound of a zipper pulled rapidly up and down. The song consists of alternating two-syllable phrases, *fee-bee, fee-bay, fee-bee, fee-bay*, at the rate of thirty phrases per minute, all delivered with clocklike regularity.

During April 2–4 it was overcast and spitting snow, and the phoebes were uncharacteristically silent. When I awoke on April 5 to find the ground covered with an inch of snow, I feared for their lives. Phoebes belong to the tyrant flycatcher family and are adapted for capturing insects on the wing. They have favorite perches from which they sally forth to snatch their airborne prey. But there had been no insects aloft for days. I was surprised to see one of the phoebes on the ground under my truck, apparently searching for insects there. I was even more struck to see one bird first hover nearby, then pick at and finally eat the suet I had hung from the porch railing for the woodpeckers. Although their predation is usually triggered by the movement of insects in flight, the phoebes had, when necessary, improvised to find new food.

The end of that week brought milder weather, and my diary indicates that the pair was present but quiet: "Only soft whisper calls near the nest." On April 9 the female, with her mate in attendance, began gathering billfuls of mud and bright green moss for the nest, making trip after trip with speed and apparent urgency. Phoebes use mud to cement their nest onto narrow structures such as a half-inch width of a board, and occasionally even manage to attach their nest to a vertical rock or cement wall, such as under a bridge.

The eggs were not laid until the last week of April, as the weather warmed up, serviceberry bloomed, and maples, poplars, birches, and beeches were leafing out. That week, five species of warblers arrived. The phoebes seemed intent and wary, the female incubating and the male aggressively guarding the nest and eggs. Males have good reason to mount a defense, and I have intervened more than once when a nest of our phoebes was threatened. One morning, when the phoebes had fallen silent, I noticed a cowbird hanging around. Brown-headed cowbirds are nest parasites, always using other birds to incubate their eggs and raise their young. I was sure the cowbird, a female, was targeting the phoebes' nest to insert an egg, and apparently the phoebes knew it too. Five minutes after the cowbird was gone, they erupted into a song that continued unabated for five minutes. Several years earlier I had removed a chipmunk that repeatedly tried to get at a phoebe nest, persisting even as the birds frantically attempted to repel it. The pair's vocal response was now similarly vigorous.

These events and the fact that the phoebes are so accustomed to our household — they don't flush from the nest even when we go in and out the squeaky door, and they use our vehicles as perches — lead me to wonder about this species' choice of nest sites. They are not only adapting to new situations but also benefiting from the human presence. Some tropical bird species rear their young near wasp nests and depend on the insects to repel predators. Perhaps humans perform the same service for phoebes.

Five young hatched in mid-May after about sixteen days of incubation. In addition to fulfilling the nestlings' demands for food, the adults kept the nest meticulously clean, at first by eating the chicks' fecal pellets and later by carrying them off for disposal far from the nest. But by the last week in May, when the young were rapidly feathering out, fecal pellets started to accumulate under the nest. That meant the chicks would soon fledge. Sure enough, on June 1, at about 6 a.m., I heard excited chirps and then saw one of the young fluttering off, with both parents accompanying it. Another chick was on the ground by the back door. I picked it up. It closed its eyes and feigned death, but when I put it on the woodpile, it quickly scampered off. By afternoon, when all was quiet around the house, I heard the adults in the nearby woods. When I investigated, I found all five young perched in a row about fifteen feet up in a leafy ironwood tree.

By the next dawn, the male was already back, singing by the house. I heard the pair's nest chatter that says, "Here is the place." With not a day wasted, the phoebes were back at the nest site! They were still feeding their fledged young, but in two more days the female had already relined the nest and started laying a second clutch of eggs. On July 11 the second brood of four nestlings fledged.*

The phoebe pair spends little time around the house after July. In mid-September we commonly hear and see the pair, but only for a day or two. As the foliage brightens and the forest turns silent, they leave. I always miss these lively housemates until they return the following spring.

---

* Later, while living in my cabin in the mountains of western Maine, where the season is shorter, the phoebes raised only one clutch per year.

Conversation with a Sapsucker

Natural History, November 2016

ONE SUMMER, I LITERALLY RAN ACROSS A WOODPECKER while out running. The bird popped up at my feet — fluttering and floundering — trying to get out of my way but unable to fly. There was obviously something wrong with it. As I picked it up to examine, it screamed loudly in protest. It was fully feathered and its garb fit that of a juvenile yellow-bellied sapsucker (*Sphyrapicus varius*). I couldn't distinguish its sex, because the red on the throat of males of this species — found even in juvenile garb — is acquired somewhat later. I found no sign of a broken wing bone or any other injury. Its keel was sharp, however, indicating that its flight muscles were atrophied. No parents were around and, likely, it had not been fed for days.

The bird's condition did not entirely surprise me. In early spring this year, the weather had been promising enough for birds to start their usual full clutches, but then there had been days of gushing rain and cold, which negatively affect insect populations. Before the rains came, there had been bumblebees (all queens), so by now I had expected an abundance of offspring — worker bees swarming over blooming fireweed, meadowsweet, milkweed, dogbane, and American chestnut trees. But instead I rarely saw even one. Bumblebees are conspicuous. Other insects, which I notice less often, must have also been affected. In any case, a link in the food chain had been broken, which would impact the birds: not all the young get fed in times of poor weather. This bird, although it had been fed enough to fledge, had then lost the strength to fly. It was doomed to starve if left where it was.

As I held it in my hands, it fluffed out its head feathers and vented vociferously. I waited for its parents to come to its cries. None came, and I had to make a decision. I could leave the bird and trot on, certain of its fate, or I could intervene. I subscribe to the *principle* that one should not "mess with nature," but reality dictated a compromise. We eat, drive cars, clear land, and build homes that disrupt entire ecosystems. Each of us necessarily has a huge impact on innumerable species. Why not help a member of another species in direct need when I had the opportunity? My act of stumbling upon the bird made the decision unavoidable. But to take this sapsucker home meant finding the proper food and a place to house it, and having the time and patience to care for it. As I held it there on the road, I could not assume anything, except the bird's impossible odds, which dictated that I could do no wrong by trying and failing. And so I took off my T-shirt and wrapped the bird in it. I still had a mile or so to run to my turnaround point, so I put the package down to pick it up on the way back, and continued, meanwhile hoping for an epiphany about how to nurse and what to feed the baby bird.

None had materialized by the time I came back, nor had the parents of this woodpecker. It was still rolled up in my shirt, and I picked it up and ran the rest of the way home. The bird squirmed now and then, but otherwise it was calm throughout the run. At home, I put it in a wooden box with screen windows that I had previously used to house caterpillars.

The sapsucker seemed calm in the box. No more struggles, no more screams. I thought I even heard a *churr* sound. I happened to have some fresh raw meat handy. Protein is protein. I held a small piece in long forceps alongside its bill. After only brief hesitation, the sapsucker took it off the forceps, swallowed, and made a couple *cheep* sounds in the process, and then started taking one piece of meat after another. An hour later, it again expressed hunger by *churr*ing. After a few more feedings, I started announcing my arrivals with my own *peep, peep, peep* sound.

Before the day was out, this sapsucker juvenile made a *churr*ing noise merely when I came to the box and opened the cover. It had learned to associate my arrival and the sound of the box opening with food delivery.

The next day, the sapsucker hopped up to the edge of the box and took meat directly from my fingers. I realized, though, that if we had been outdoors, the situation would have been very different. Years ago, when I was studying ravens, which are so wild in Maine that they fly away at the sight of a human, I was surprised to see them feed from my hand after capture. However, after equipping them with radio transmitters, wing tags, or leg bands and releasing them, they only moments later behaved exactly as they had before capture; context is everything.

By the second day, the sapsucker fed at fairly regular two-hour intervals. It was recovering rapidly, faster than I realized. After one feeding of several pieces of steak, it suddenly flew off the box and out the door, which had been left open. I thought my rescue experiment was not yet over because the bird was not able to fly well enough to cope in the wild. Accipiter hawks specialize in catching young birds. It seemed doomed after all. However, hours later I heard *churr*ing in the grass in our field. The bird had generated enough power to gain distance but not enough to attain altitude. I knew it had not run out of fuel — hit the wall, or the bonk, in marathon runners' terms — because it had been feeding steadily earlier in the day. I had witnessed bird-bonking the previous winter when a downy woodpecker arrived at our feeder so weak that it could barely fly. After refueling on suet taken from my fingers after I had grabbed it, it revived and flew off. That was not the case with this young sapsucker; it had not yet regained its flight muscles. I recaptured it with a butterfly net and brought it back to the box. This time, as I held it in my hands, it neither struggled nor screamed and eagerly resumed taking meat from my fingers.

The changed behavior made me wonder if the bird "knew" I had rescued it — not necessarily in a conscious way, of course — but it may have felt the contrast from its days of starving to being regularly fed, and it may have associated the new with what made the difference. Such apparent appreciation of riches has been seen in the response of dogs and cats that have been rescued. Animals accept the status quo, almost whatever it is. But they respond to a change, even a small one, from what they were used to.

After another day of devouring hefty portions of meat, the sapsucker again flew out the door. This time it gained enough height to disappear into the foliage of maple trees in the nearby woods. Although it had gained much strength, its flight was still clumsy. It had returned to the woods of bird song, squirrel chatter, and tree frog calls, but its chances of survival still seemed slight.

Just before dark that day I made my *peep, peep, peep* calls at the edge of the woods. I had no idea where the bird was, or even if it was still near. Almost instantly, it replied with its own *churr* call from in the woods. I quickly procured gobbets of meat and replied with more *peep, peep, peep* calls — the code for both food and "I am here." The sapsucker then flew from the woods and landed on the branch of a maple tree a meter above my head. It hopped down the tree trunk to pluck the piece of meat from my fingers, and then hopped back up and settled under a thick limb. It was still there later that night when I got up and checked with a flashlight. The next morning I found it still there at 4:30 a.m. A half-hour later, it landed on our cabin wall, making its usual call announcing its presence, signaling to me that it wanted food. I went out and complied.

Our conversations became routine. A week into our relationship, the sapsucker again landed on the cabin wall below my window and announced its arrival. I went out, and it now landed on my hand. When I lifted it to my face, the bird plucked food from between my teeth. In spite of this close contact, I was confident there was no danger of it becoming dependent on me because it had constant access to the wild. And indeed, the woodpecker was already visiting us less and less frequently.

The next day, I spotted a sapsucker in juvenile plumage at an ant trail on the trunk of the large birch tree next to the cabin. It was picking off ants in the same manner, seemingly, as the adults I had routinely watched there. To test if it was my sapsucker, so to speak, I gave my *peep, peep, peep.* The answer was clear, though rather feeble, a barely audible *churr.* And then it paid no attention to me. I was still skeptical that it could be my bird because I had never before had a sapsucker give a response like that. When I sidled up to it at the tree trunk — with my head within a meter

— rather than fly off, it made one more faint *churr* and then left; there was no more doubt what bird it was.

After that encounter, the sapsucker continued to visit occasionally but showed no interest in anything I offered nor in approaching me. It had no more need of me, and had perhaps found food that it preferred over steak. It acted as though it had forgotten me, or else it had switched to its adult behavior.

It had been a week of conversation with a sapsucker, but then it ended, as if by the flip of a switch. I had communicated with a wild woodpecker. I learned at least two of its signals, a vocabulary of two words. Their meaning varied with context and with intensity and repetition. The first, the *churr*, was a one-syllable call of an upward, inflected high pitch that trailed downward. The bird gave it when it came to the cabin to be fed. Given the context, it translates to "feed me" but also to "I am here." At first daylight every morning when I went out and called, the sapsucker replied with a single *churr* from wherever it was in the nearby woods, but it did not necessarily come. I had heard this call for years and had never given it a thought. The *churr* call was not just a juvenile begging, because the sapsucker did not always come after it had told me where it was (a parent might have gone to it). Furthermore, the *churr* was not just a reply to my *peep, peep, peep*. The bird used it as a summons or solicitation, one it gave after it had come to the cabin spontaneously without my calling it, usually after landing on the door or by a window.

The sapsucker's *cheep*ing vocalization was almost continuous while it was being fed — the same sound one hears from a nest hole with hungry chicks, where the volume increases greatly when a parent arrives. Since the birds are already aware a parent or feeder is near and about to deliver the food, why *cheep* at all and why make it louder? I suspect it is a signal of hunger to the adult, but it may also serve to "cheer on" the adult for bringing the food. Increased volume of the *cheep* may signal a greater hunger and give the loudest nestling a competitive edge over its siblings to end up receiving more of the incoming food.

The sapsucker is now independent. It could have continued to take the food I provided, but it chose not to. A switch had occurred as though by a decision. Forgetting could have been part of it, a useful if not adaptive trait. Brain space is not unlimited. A woodpecker needs to be efficient; it must get everything right in

Yellow-bellied sapsucker at his sap-lick made in a birch tree, along with others taking advantage of it.

life in a couple of weeks, not years. It needs to have major adaptive traits ready for immediate functioning. The bird's change in behavior toward me seemed like the usual parting of ways with parents. Rationally, I was glad for it, but emotionally, I missed the relationship. A woodpecker is not a social animal, but we humans are. We bond to what we become close to, in this case the young sapsucker, but we also bond to our surroundings — the nature this bird represented.

Hawk Watching

Outside, Fall 1998

EVERY APRIL SINCE I WAS A KID, A PAIR OF GOSHAWKS HAS built its nest in a dense grove of pines on Picker Hill, near our family farm in Maine. Our family has had a long relationship with this pair. More than once I remember my mother stomping out of the house with a shotgun in hand when one of the hawks came to perch in the big elm from which it eyed the chickens in the yard. In spite of my mother's vigilance, the hawks eventually caught most of her pigeons, but that was after the story I'm about to tell.

I got to know these goshawks personally. They once touched me, and rather indelicately — with their thin, lemon-yellow scaled toes tipped with inch-long curved blue toenails sharp as knives. I had made the mistake of climbing their nest tree. Suddenly I heard loud clanging calls like the banging of metal pots. Then a second one started in. And then I noticed the bright-red eyes of the huge white-breasted hawk staring at me from the dead branch of a neighboring pine. Our eyes locked, and at that moment I heard a swoosh and in the same instant also felt the impact as the other bird hit me on the back and its talons raked across my spine. I realized then that *Accipiter gentilis* is not all that the name implies — either that or Carolus Linnaeus, the great Swedish biologist who had named the species, had a perverse sense of humor. Later that summer, when I saw the hawks try to get a meal for their young, they won even more of my respect. It was then that I pleaded with my mother to please lay down her shotgun for good.

I happened to be crossing the hayfield in back of our house on a slightly overcast day in July. The starling young were long out of their nest and had joined up into flocks for protection. One of these flocks of about fifty birds was flying over, and I looked up and saw a goshawk rapidly approaching from the direction of

Egg and just-hatched chick of a broad-winged hawk, with a green fern frond that it had just inserted into the nest.

Picker Hill. The great hawk was gaining height, rapidly pumping its short, broad wings. The starlings saw it too, and they converged into a tight group. No individual stood out. They were safe now, I thought.

The goshawk had gained about a hundred feet of altitude above the starlings, which were now streaking off toward Pease Pond. Starlings are swift flyers, and the goshawk is not built for a prolonged high-speed chase. It is a forest bird with stubby wings, adept at quick maneuvers through the trees, using its long tail as a rudder.

The hawk's wings paused as it angled down and then plunged like a rock, right at the starlings. In only a second or two it was just above and behind the panicked birds, and I knew it would miss. But then the starlings also dove. The hawk's plunge was faster, and when the goshawk was directly under the flock, it flipped upside down and spread out its wings. One of the diving starlings fell into those same yellow talons that had raked my back. The goshawk then flipped back up and flapped off toward Picker Hill with its prize. I was left standing open-mouthed with amazement at the power and grace of the show.

As I walked across the hayfield that day, I had not expected to see such a sight, nor could I have predicted from my previous encounters that goshawks are capable of so magnificent a feat. I presume that the nearly fifty starlings that were spared felt relief, maybe even joy.

You wouldn't think that seeing a chicken hawk kill a songbird would be much to marvel about. But there it was — I saw a goshawk kill a starling, and it set my limbic system pumping.

Kinglets' Realm of Cold

Natural History, February 1993

The problem of how kinglets could possibly survive long winter nights was to me an incredible enigma, which provoked me to write Winter World. *At the end of the book I still had only a hypothesis of how it might be possible. But subsequently I found proof of it. I here present an essay I wrote in the midst of wonder, ten years before the book was published, and then ten years before I found the proof, as described at the end of this essay.*

ON A MIDWINTER NIGHT IN THE MOUNTAINS OF WESTERN Maine, the spruce-fir forest sounds like giant pounding surf as the wind drives thick snow through the trees. The thermometer reads minus 20 degrees F, and bodily contact with the biting air can be lethal to human and bird alike.

I'm clothed in insulated long underwear, wool pants covered by ski pants, two sweaters, a windbreaker, a woolen cap, gloves with liners, wool stockings, and insulated boots. My hands would be immobilized and useless in less than a minute if I took off my gloves. I'd be shivering violently if I stood still for only a few minutes, and my body temperature would begin to drop unless I kept moving vigorously as well. How do the resident birds maintain a body temperature several degrees higher than ours, even for a minute? More amazingly, how do they survive the entire night?

Ruffed grouse escape the biting air by diving directly into the deep snow, hollowing out a temporary shelter for the night. Chickadees and nuthatches seek refuge in ready-made tree holes and hollows. Downy and hairy woodpeckers excavate tree holes in November, apparently for the sole purpose of sleeping in them at night. The ornithologist Charles Kendeigh has shown that sleeping in cavities can aid overnight survival because heat is retained near the bird, and considerable energy is saved from the reduced need for shivering. Chickadees, as shown by the biologist Susan Chaplin, also save energy by allowing their body temperature to decline by some 18 degrees F. Most seed-eating birds, including pine and evening grosbeaks, crossbills, redpolls, goldfinches, and pine siskins, show little nocturnal torpor, and they tarry in these Maine winter woods only if their respective food trees bear ample seeds packed with enough fat to fuel their nearly constant shivering throughout the night. The key to survival is food, because food is converted to heat through shivering. When food is scarce and shivering not viable, the bird may resort to torpor by turning down the body's thermostat.

In a few days, the storm is almost forgotten. For the survivors, life returns to their usual routine. The grouse feed on birch buds, the finches fly in flocks from one seed-bearing tree to another, and the pileated woodpecker again hammers long and deep oval cavities into the bases of fir trees to extract hibernating carpenter ants.

Above the raucous *kek-kek-kek* of the pileated woodpecker

and the *tsee-tsee* of the chickadee, I hear a faint conversation of golden-crowned kinglets in a spruce thicket. Their sound is as unobtrusive as a gentle breeze and just as easily goes unnoticed by all except those who know it. Among the thick branches, the tiny birds climb, hop, and hover as they forage, mainly on the undersides of twigs. Plumaged in soft olive, these birds have crowns of gold bordered in black. The males also have a flamelike orange crest, which is normally concealed among yellow crown feathers but can instantly be erected. The golden-crowned kinglet inhabits the coniferous forests of the northern United States and Canada year-round. (A related species, the ruby-crowned kinglet, is here only in the summer.)

Awed by their achievement of overnight survival in the cold, I wanted to find out where the birds sleep. Evening shadows were already falling at 4:30 p.m., when the three birds I was following suddenly made long, high-pitched calls, flew off as if on signal, and vanished. Once again I was unable to find where or how they spent the night. However, the survivors of the storm a few nights earlier lingered in my mind.

The presence of kinglets in an area with recurrent subzero frosts is remarkable on at least two counts. First, the birds are tiny. At about two ounces, they are among the smallest passerine, or perching, birds in the world, only slightly heavier than most hummingbirds. A kinglet's body, without its feathers, is no larger than the end of one's little finger. But kinglets maintain a high body temperature, just like other perching birds, even when air temperatures dip to minus 30 degrees F or colder. Some fifty years ago, the Finnish ornithologist Pontus Palmgren determined that the gold crest, or European, kinglet maintains a body temperature of 103–107 degrees F in winter and is insulated with feathers accounting for 23–25 percent of its body weight.

According to the physical laws of heating and cooling, a two-ounce kinglet should lose heat at a rate about 75 percent faster than a four-ounce chickadee, and would have to consume and burn 75 percent more food per unit of body mass to maintain the same body temperature. Also, since smaller birds have a lesser absolute amount of insulation than larger ones, they cool even faster than predicted by body mass alone. Nonetheless, golden-crowned kinglets survive in cold climates alongside the raven, the world's largest songbird.

A second notable fact about kinglets' winter residence in Maine is that they feed on insects. In the fall, most insectivorous birds migrate south, seeking better hunting grounds. In contrast, many seed eaters stay. How do kinglets consume, as they must, up to three times their own body weight in insects each short winter day? Unlike chickadees, kinglets never come to feeders for seeds and suet. If kinglets are without food for only one or two hours in the daytime, they starve to death. Yet in the north, where they live and appear to prosper, winter nights are generally fifteen hours long. Since foraging is not possible at night, and kinglets have not been observed to cache food, what saves them from dying during the night?

In studies of the closely related gold crest, researchers concluded that in winter the birds specialize to feed on collembolans, or springtails. A species of these primitive insects, commonly known as "snow fleas," is abundant in the Maine woods, and I determined that some may spend their time on trees in the winter. Might they be the manna on which the kinglets subsist? I examined the stomach contents of a dead kinglet at dusk. Temperatures over the previous two weeks had been steadily below 0 degrees F. The kinglet's stomach was filled to capacity: it contained the remains of thirty-nine geometrid caterpillars, a spider, a few moth scales, twenty-four almost microscopic fly larvae, and just four springtails.

While this probe showed that springtails are not the birds' only food in Maine, it failed to solve the mystery of the kinglets' survival here. Although the bird's stomach was packed with food, it could have fueled heat projection for hardly more than an hour or so on a cold night. Could most of the kinglets' energy come from fat stores laid down throughout the day?

Charles R. Blem and John F. Pagels at Virginia Commonwealth University assayed body composition of golden-crowned kinglets throughout the daylight period in midwinter in Virginia. Body fat reserves increased from a low of about 0.2 grams in the morning to about 0.6 grams in the evening. Lipids have a high energy content, but using the standard equations for maintenance metabolism of birds of this size, Blem and Pagels predicted that a kinglet at a normal body temperature accumulates no more than *half* the stores of lipid needed to fuel its metabolism through fifteen hours of night, even at a modest 32 degrees F. Therefore, the fat stores accumulated during the day are not enough to keep a kinglet warm even on a relatively mild winter night. However, Ellen Thaler and her coworkers at the Alpenzoo in Innsbruck, Austria, after observing a slight difference in the body weight of a bird between dusk and dawn, calculated that if this weight loss is due to fat utilization, then energy reserves would suffice even at minus 13 degrees F during an eighteen-hour nocturnal fast. However, the nocturnal weight loss is almost certainly not from fat alone, because the birds also lose weight from gut-emptying, as well as loss of glycogen, protein, and water.

Despite the unsolved problem of their overnight energy source and their food supply, the kinglets' survival strategies undoubtedly include mechanisms of energy conservation seen in other birds.

Kinglets conserve some body heat by puffing out their feathers and tucking in their twiglike legs and feet.* Do kinglets also stretch fat and energy supplies to last the whole night by becoming torpid? During torpor, the animal turns down its internal thermostat, and nocturnal torpor is generally a function of body size. The smaller the animal, the more energy it saves by hypothermia, and the faster it can again warm up in the morning. Some hummingbirds go torpid regularly at night in the summer. A logical prediction would be that torpor is a key adaptation of kinglets in winter, yet all the data so far available indicate that they do not go into torpor at night. Thaler, who has long studied kinglets in captivity, found from her measurements of body temperature in outdoor aviaries that no steep drop in nighttime body temperature occurs.

Perhaps studies of wild birds, or of birds without access to ample aviary diets, will shed more light on this possibility. In terms of saving energy, it makes sense to enter torpor. But I suspect it is dangerous to let body temperature drop if temperatures get too low: a small, cooled bird might be unable to regain thermal control at a low body temperature, and would then freeze within minutes when air temperature dips below minus 15 degrees F.

Behavior is also crucial in achieving nocturnal energy balance. Naturalists have observed that winter birds are almost absurdly tame at very low temperatures; they become oblivious to distractions and even to predators. So too with kinglets. They spend less time avoiding predators, moving about, and aggressively displaying, and more time concentrating on feeding.

Another critical behavioral response is finding a good nocturnal shelter, which is why I had on numerous attempts tried to fol-

---

* Counter-current heat exchangers play a prominent role in maintaining blood circulation through the extremities.

low the birds at dusk to find out where they come to rest. We knew almost nothing about where wild kinglets spend the night, except that they likely seek shelter in dense conifer branches. Even a little shelter may make the difference between death and survival when near the edge. Do kinglets preferentially perch in the lower portions of thick trees where there is less wind current and convection? Do they fly to a preselected safe place, such as up against a baffle of the wind, and suddenly disappear out of sight at dusk, explaining why even my best efforts to follow them to their overnight resting place are thwarted? Blem observed these sudden departures too, and claimed to have seen a kinglet enter a squirrel's nest at dusk. I had once seen kinglets disappear at dusk into a thick conifer containing a squirrel's nest, but would not have been able to determine whether it entered the nest there or just perched next to it. Squirrel nests have hidden and closed entrances, and I was skeptical that a kinglet would be able to find or force its way in, take the chance of doing so, or be tolerated if it did. Squirrels are major predators of eggs and young nesting birds.

There is no doubt, though, that a critical aspect of the micro-environment where kinglets spend the night is the availability of other warm bodies of their own kind. Studies have shown that at 32 degrees F, pairs of roosting European gold crests reduce their heat loss by 23 percent, and trios reduce heat loss by about 37 percent.

Just before dark, European gold crests form groups with the aid of contact calls. Thaler observed that when approaching their sleeping tree, the birds make specific calls, which presumably attract the members of the troop, a number of kinglets foraging together. A second assembly, or bunching, call draws the group into a cluster along a horizontal branch where they will spend the night. Birds in the center of clusters sit bunched with their head pulled in to their shoulders and their bill pointing up, while the birds at the edges hold their head to the side. The contact groups form in warm weather as well as cold, but whereas it may take them twenty minutes to get into position in warm weather, they bunch up in only five minutes when it is cold. Mated pairs always bunch up with each other in mere seconds in cold weather, as do siblings. The raven, in the same climate, survives by sharing food in the form of large carcasses. The kinglet, in contrast, probably survives by sharing warmth. In both species, sharing is motivated by the immediate need to get access to either food or warmth. Since one is converted to the other, food and warmth are functionally similar.

In summer, kinglets tend to be common throughout their range, but in winter, they are sometimes common, sometimes rare, or even absent. No reason for this winter variation of abundance has been found. Perhaps major portions of the population die off every winter when the weather becomes particularly bitter. Heavy winter losses could be counterbalanced by the exceptional numbers of young that kinglets produce each year. Every year a pair produces two clutches, each clutch containing seven to twelve young. (Pairs usually build their second nest before the first clutch has fledged.) Thus, only a small fraction of winter survivors could account for a substantial new population the next fall.

I was curious to find out if, in the minus 20 degrees F temperature, the kinglets near my Maine camp had survived. In the twenty-six total hours that I looked for them in February and March, I encountered eighteen of them (in seven troops). I doubt that I overlooked any kinglets nearby, because the birds vocalize almost constantly. Their thin bell-like *cheep*s reminded me of small pebbles being struck together, and on the still and windless days when I searched for the birds, I could hear them from at least twenty paces. One bird traveling alone made sixty-six faint calls in one minute, while kinglets traveling in groups of two called, on average, only forty times per minute. Finally, a threesome that had joined a noisy troop of more than twenty black-capped chickadees called only about two times a minute each. My skimpy probe does not provide sufficient data for conclusions, but it does open the question of what role this vocal behavior plays in kinglets' winter survival.

In early March, the average number of kinglets per troop near my camp was only 2.6. If huddling is necessary for survival over cold nights, then these Maine birds didn't seem to have many spare huddlers nearby. Body warmers are not likely to appear magically just at dusk. Perhaps the kinglets' sociability throughout the day helps ensure the presence of huddlers on cold nights. Attracting and keeping contact with others may be a key component of winter survival, one that is not likely to be maintained by vision alone in the dense coniferous forests. With an average of only 2.6 birds per troop, losing even one more member might doom the rest during the next period of heavy frost or food deprivation. Silent birds will not be followed — they must follow others (which could take time from their precious foraging) or become isolated. By calling, they can both follow and be followed.

Knowing that these wraiths of the forest were still here despite the subzero weather was reassuring. But as I retired to the warmth of my cabin the night of March 3, I again heard gusts of wind that moaned through the woods and shook the cabin. Rain pummeled the roof all night. Bone dry under three blankets, I wondered how the kinglets were faring.

When I awoke the next morning, realizing that there was still at least a month of winter ahead, I heard the trees creaking. They were glazed in ice. The freezing rain continued throughout the day; the tree limbs drooped lower and lower until many came crashing down to the ground. Would the birds still be there next week?

On March 17, I was finally reassured that they would again populate the summer woods. The sun shone, and the snow, still two feet deep in some spots, was heavily crusted and easy to walk on. Woodpeckers drummed, and two ravens careened in a wild chase over the valley. Then I heard the song of a golden-crowned kinglet, a rapid cascade of a dozen pure, vibrant notes crammed into a mere second and repeated six to nine times a minute. The kinglets' time for courtship had returned. Despite early April snowstorms, the kinglets' deep nest cups of fine moss and lichens, cobwebs, and snowshoe hare fur would again be made high in the spruce boughs and filled with two layers of tiny eggs.

CODA

Theory guides, but I prefer facts. In *Winter World*, I reviewed facts, and ended the book with the following sentence: "I will continue to marvel and wonder how the little feather puffs are faring. They defy the odds and the laws of physics, and prove that the fabulous is possible."

I had followed these northern kinglets again and again, and hadn't found out how they spent their nights, although I had observed that they foraged into the gloaming, well past the time of day when other songbirds retire. But late one winter evening, a month or so after *Winter World* was published, I again saw a flock of kinglets foraging at dusk, and one after another flew into a small pine tree. It seemed isolated enough from other trees, and late enough for them to possibly stay, so I thought I might be able to determine if none flew out. I waited and watched carefully, and to my excitement saw none fly out. I returned long after dark, hoping they would be sound asleep. I ascended the tree with great care, and searching with a flashlight, found a four-pack of them — with their heads to the middle and their four tails sticking out of one composite fluff-ball. They were alert; one poked its head out and looked around. It seemed oblivious or indifferent to the beam of light and stuck its head back into the cluster. This heads-up confirmed that this bird was not in torpor; its body temperature was still elevated. With increased caution, I crept closer and was able to photograph the four-pack of huddled golden-crowned kinglets. The image may not be my highest-quality photography, but it is my most prized snapshot. It has emotion; it tells a tale. It is high-quality documented proof (published in 2004 in the *Wilson Bulletin*) of why little golden-crowned kinglets stick together in winter: they are one another's shelter. They can spend a longer day foraging because at the very last minute, in a flash, they snuggle into the warmth and comfort of home.

The Diabolical Nightjar

Natural History, July–August 2017

I'M USUALLY MOTIVATED BY DIRECT EXPERIENCE, BUT THIS time motivation came from viewing a photograph of two nightjars perched on the ground. They looked like the whip-poor-will of North America, but these were diabolical nightjars of Indonesia. I was intrigued because the two were so close to each other that they were touching, an enigmatic behavior because nightjars, birds of the night, are solitary, and this species was known as one of the rarest bird species on earth.

The photograph was in a book review written by N. J. Collar and published in *Kukila*, the journal of Indonesian ornithology. I had read it in 2010, where I first saw the image captured on camera by someone named Yong Ding Li in June 2007. Li happened to be at the right spot at the right time with a camera, in Lore Lindu National Park in Sulawesi. His photo was of the diabolical nightjars, one of several bird species discussed in the reviewed book (*The Snoring Bird*, which happened to be mine, and about my father, Gerd Heinrich, who had discovered the diabolical nightjar

— also officially known as Heinrich's nightjar — in 1931; it was not seen again until 1996).

Nightjars typically lay two eggs, so the two birds in the photograph could potentially have been the young of a nest. But from their plumage they seemed adult, and if adult, then they were likely mates — but even so, why would they be pressed next to each other? Since they were in the hot lowland tropics, they could not have been huddling for warmth, so why were they doing it? With nothing more to go on except the knowledge that this was an extremely rare bird, I filed the image away as a faint memory of an interesting anecdote, and left it at that. But a year later the potential enigma came back to me, this time on a Christmas card sent to me by someone in Alberta, Canada, someone whom I had also never met.

The card was decorated with a photograph of the same extremely rare species, the same diabolical nightjar of Sulawesi, except that the signer of the card, M. P. Marklevitz, referred to it by the third of its three names, the satanic nightjar. This photograph was taken in the same nature reserve as the other, and like the other photograph, it also showed *two* of the birds perched next to each other on the ground. This photograph, though, had been taken more from the top than with a head-on view, so the birds' elongate tails were clearly visible — they were definitely adults! Thus, these were likely a mated pair, and Mr. M. Patrick Marklevitz wrote me, "I managed to locate and photograph two pairs in the upper reaches of Lore Lindu Park." Again paired? What amazing coincidences, I thought, and the wonder increased, although I still saw no opportunity nor had the wish to travel to Sulawesi to track down such a rare bird in the jungle. But the images of it did not go away.

Marklevitz's photo showed what I inferred might have been a third bird, possibly young, partially covered by the pair. It was either this (such ground-nesting birds have young that closely match their background of leaves and other debris) or I had been fooled by a fortuitous arrangement of dry leaves that created a Rorschach illusion in my mind. To find out which, I tracked Marklevitz down several years later (through his internet presence as a nature photographer), to try to find out more about his nightjar photograph. He led me to exactly what I had needed to see: a website, "Oriental Bird Images," that turned out to be a treasure-trove of information collected over decades by dedicated bird watchers. And so, now seven years later, I was suddenly provided much more information than I could ever have dreamed possible.

On this website, I viewed hundreds of photographs posted of Indonesian nightjars, birds of the genus *Caprimulgus* (fifteen species) and *Eurostopodus* or eared nightjars (three species). I viewed a total of 294 photos of roosting birds (excluding photos of flying birds, multiple photos of the same birds, and portraits). Twenty of these photos were of the diabolical nightjar, and seven were photos of pairs, whereas within the 274 remaining of other nightjars, there had been only one with two birds in the same frame. That is, unless in the unlikely event that birders deliberately desisted from photographing single birds of the diabolical, then pair roosting is an overwhelmingly favored behavior by this specific species.

The photographs were from all over Indonesia, and all of the twenty photographs of the diabolical were taken in the Lore Lindu Park in north-central Sulawesi.* I also Googled "pair-roosting nightjars" and found five videos and five photographs of the Trin-

_____

* The only record of this bird outside this nature reserve is the original female type specimen discovered in 1931, collected at 250 meters' elevation in the forest near Kumaresot, at the foot of the Kelabat Volcano, in the Minahassa Province of northern Sulawesi.

idad white-tailed nightjar (*Caprimulgus cayennensis*), photographs of the blackish nightjar (*C. nigrescens*) and the collared nightjar (*C. enarratus*) from Madagascar, but none in pairs.

Why would the satanic nightjar stay paired up and close together? Staying together would promote monogamy, but in many birds, that is achieved or maintained secondarily by site-fidelity. Staying wedded next to each other seemed like potentially extreme monogamy. Is it selected because under some conditions it provides insurance for having a suitable mate handy?

Such monogamy might become crucial where the population is especially sparse or the breeding season extremely short. It might also be necessary where the annual ritual of courting is costly. When a species becomes rare and the ability for individuals to find a mate becomes a factor limiting reproduction, the species might distribute itself increasingly more locally into specific localities. The current conservation status of this diabolical nightjar is "vulnerable," and it is indeed listed as a "restricted range species." These descriptive labels would have applied to this species already nearly a century ago, and may to its current rarity.

My father, with his wife, Anneliese, and her sister Liselotte as bird preparators, discovered this nightjar in 1931, only after they had explored and collected all over Sulawesi (then Celebes) for two years. They secured their single specimen at the very end of their bird-collecting expedition, financed by the American Museum of Natural History in New York. The enterprise had been instigated by Leonard Sanford of that museum, and Erwin Stresemann, then the world's premier ornithologist, at the Museum of Natural History in Berlin. The museums had tasked the expedition with the special mission of bringing back a rail, *Aramidopsis plateni*, that was thought to be extinct, but was rediscovered in 1932 after a two-year search. It was known only from the remains of one specimen.

The crew had been trying to resurrect this rail to please their sponsors. By the time their two years were up, the long-lost and long-sought rail that they would later refer to as *der Vogel Schnarch* (the snoring bird), after later hearing its call, had by then still not turned up — but a shipment of their bird catch had reached Berlin. Stresemann, on examining it, reported back that it contained "fantastic discoveries." One of the major ones was this nightjar.

The discoveries from the Minahassa area induced Stresemann to contact the American Natural History Museum's noted philanthropist Richard Archbold about donating another $10,000 to keep the expedition going.*

Stresemann had described the nightjar, and therefore had the honor and task of naming it. For a species name he chose *diabolicus*. Hence the common name of diabolical nightjar. His rationale for inventing the name may never be known, but I suspect he may have implied, tongue-in-cheek, that devilish forces had been at work to produce this totally unexpected rare and precious new bird, only because of his and Sanford's efforts to get the crew to stay on beyond the scheduled time to find the rail with the snoring call.

As reported by K. David Bishop and Jared M. Diamond in 1997, who then called it Heinrich's nightjar, the bird was not rediscovered until May 1996, and in the previously mentioned Lore Lindu National Park. This apparently highly local distribution (or a hot spot for birders seeking to add it to their life list?) is some eight hundred kilometers from the site of its original discovery sixty-

---

* Which finally yielded *a pair* of the seemingly extinct rail, *Aramidopsis plateni*. On catching the first one, Gerd pronounced it "the most priceless catch that I have ever hunted or will hunt."

three years earlier, where it has so far not been recorded again. Its rarity and restricted range are apparently real, and sustained isolation for long periods of time would predictably give a reproductive advantage to individuals who, if they are so fortunate to find a mate, stay together.

MAMMALS

Hidden Sweets

Previously published as "Nutcracker Sweets," *Natural History*, February 1991

THE NORTH WINDOW OF MY CAMP IN THE MAINE WOODS looks out over a long-abandoned apple orchard that is being overtaken by rapidly growing hardwoods, predominantly red and sugar maples. The forest reclaims the land quickly here, and I wage a continual battle to maintain a clearing for space and sunlight near the cabin. In thinning out the young trees, I had often selectively favored the sugar maples, which I hope to tap someday. Little did I know, until one winter day, that my saplings were already being tapped.

I had been outside watching ravens, but as is often the case, what is most interesting is often the unexpected. On this gorgeous late January afternoon, after a night of about 5 degrees F, my eye caught a red squirrel (*Tamiasciurus hudsonicus*) making rounds among the maple saplings, scampering up and down young trees in succession. Sunlight reflected off the deep snow onto the smooth tan tree bark. The weather was ideal, I thought, for sugaring, envi-

American red squirrel, Tamiasciurus hudsonicus, *collecting syrup evaporated from a bite it had previously made through the thin bark of a young sugar maple tree.*

sioning my future fun, but the season was about a month too early. Most sugarers don't tap until the end of February or early March. Most, that is, except perhaps the red squirrel I was watching. Was it actually nibbling a branch?

Now that the squirrel had my attention, I saw that it not only dashed up and down the trees but also made regular stops. It paused at dark, wet streaks visible against the dry, light bark of sugar maple saplings, then slowly worked its way up the streak, licking along the way with its little pink tongue. By now I was more than attentive; I was fascinated.

At least one red squirrel near the cabin had long been habituated to me. Indeed, the previous summer one reared a litter of young in one of my birdhouses. Red squirrels were generally a nuisance around the cabin because they pulled the chinking out from between the logs, to use for lining their nests. My repeated attempts to shoo them away had small effect, except to embolden them. I've merely taught them that I'm harmless despite my blustering. Now this squirrel's tameness allowed me to observe its eagerness and concentration as it went from one maple tree to another.

Watching from as close as six feet, I saw the squirrel's bright-pink tongue lick furiously up one streak. Then the animal scurried up to the next or scrambled headfirst down the sapling to bound in a beeline on to other trees. I was reminded of a kid gone wild in a candy store, an apt analogy, as it turned out. Were the squirrels — I soon saw three — really tapping maple trees, or were they just drinking sap because it happened to be dripping from wounds where branches had broken during storms?

My ignorance of squirrel behavior turned out to be an asset, since it allowed me to ask this naive question. Had I been more aware of the scientific literature on red squirrels, I may have dismissed what I had seen as nothing but the lapping of sap, and would have forgotten about it. But as it was, I was prepared to investigate further.

I later learned that the red squirrel had long been known to take tree sap. In 1929, Robert T. Hatt, in his detailed account of this animal, stated that red squirrels take sap as it flows from injured limbs, from sapsucker holes, and even from incisions made by the squirrels themselves. Hatt also quoted the naturalist M. A. Walton (1903) on his favorite red squirrel:

Every spring Bismarck taps the trees around my cabin. He begins on the maples and ends later on the birches. If the tree is small he taps the trunk, if large, he works the limbs. He gnaws through the bark and into the wood, then clings to the limb or trunk below the wound while he laps the sweet sap. If there is a hollow in the bark into which the sap flows, Bismarck is sure to find it.

Numerous other, although much less lengthy and detailed, accounts contained anecdotal references to red squirrels "tapping" trees or "lapping sap." In a treatise on the red squirrel's biology written in 1954, James N. Layne states that "the utilization of sap may be important during periods when water is not available in the habitat."

However, the idea that the squirrels were lapping sap for the water was not high on my list of possible explanations for the behavior I was seeing. To be sure, the water content of maple sap is usually at least 98 percent, but when the sap runs in New England, water is not a scarce commodity for winter-active animals because snow and meltwater are everywhere. If the squirrels wanted water to quench their thirst, why would they bother to go to all the trouble of climbing tree after tree and running long distances over the crusted snow to reach them? They have all the water they need directly under their feet.

I assumed instead that the squirrels were harvesting sugar as an energy source. Having long been interested in animal energetics, I could not envision them going to all this trouble to get energy by ingesting a tasteless (in my opinion) solution that is 98 percent water. Squirrels like high-energy foods. (Sap from even the best trees, generally those growing in the open and having a large crown, is not useful as food energy until extensive boiling drives off most of the water. Federal regulations stipulate that a product labeled maple syrup be at least 66 percent sugar, in this case, sucrose. Vermont stipulates that Vermont maple syrup be at least 66.9 percent sugar.) According to the studies of Christopher Smith at the University of Kansas, a red squirrel requires a minimum daily energy budget of about 117,000 calories. I calculated that if a squirrel were to meet this requirement by drinking sap, it would have to drink at least forty gallons per day. Clearly, this exceeds any squirrel's drinking capacity. The more I tried to fathom the squirrels' behavior, the more engrossed I became.

Assuming as I did that the animals were collecting sugar rather than water, how did they identify sugar maples, and how did they solve the problem of deriving sugar from the sap? Near my cabin, there were some twenty species of common trees, yet the squirrels visited only two, the red and sugar maples. Red maple sap is about twice as dilute as that of the sugar maple, and the squirrels clearly preferred the sugar maples over the red, and both over all others.

The next problem, perhaps less daunting given a set of sharp incisors, is to gain access to the sap. In most trees, some fluid can be obtained by nicking the cambium layer of the bark. In the maples, however, the sugar-bearing tissue is not within the inner bark but in the woody xylem beneath it. That is why sugar farmers bore their trees to a depth of three inches. Simply removing a bit of bark from a maple in winter does not yield sap, as I found out, to my surprise, while trying to replicate the squirrels' seemingly shallow taps.

Another problem faced by a potential sugar harvester is the timing of the sap run. Through long experience and, more recently, through detailed scientific investigations, humans now know that the maple sap run is triggered, and in part sustained, by large temperature fluctuations. The sap runs in the trees in winter, early spring, and, to a lesser extent, in the fall, when there are frosts at night followed by elevated daytime temperatures. However, the sap runs cease before or when buds start to open, even if frosts persist.

Given the various peculiarities of the availability and the timing of the sap flow, harvesting maple sugar would seem to demand a specialized suite of evolved behaviors, rather than mere opportunism. Lapping up raw sap randomly oozing out of a tree to satisfy thirst is one thing, but it is quite another to harvest the sugar found in maple sap so that it can be an energy gain and not a drain. These thoughts induced me to make systematic observations.

The sap streaks that the squirrels were feeding from looked glistening and dark against the bark. Superficially, they looked like streaks of water. Closer examination, however, revealed otherwise. One day when the sap was running vigorously, I measured the sugar concentration at sixty taps with my pocket refractometer, a tool normally used by beer and wine makers (but one that I utilized to examine flower nectar when studying bumblebees and their foraging behavior). At the few taps made on horizontal branches, sap collected in droplets on the bottom of the branch before dripping to the ground. Sap from these taps was 4 to 5 percent sugar. This is an unusually high content for raw sap, but it is still a rather weak drink. At most taps, however, the sap ran down in thin streaks, averaging some sixteen inches long, along a slanting branch or upright trunk. Here, the sap was "captured" by the surface tension of the bark, and like a continually drying wick, the bark spread the sap over a large surface area suitable for rapid evaporation. The sugar concentration on these streaks, where the

syrup had nearly dried to produce a sticky glaze, was almost uniformly above 6 percent, and in some cases reaching over 55 percent, the upper limit for readings on my instrument. The squirrels
I observed fed almost exclusively on the concentrated streaks, using their teeth as well as their tongues, biting off the sugar along
with a thin coating of the bark adhering to it, seemingly avoiding
the runny, dilute sap drips.

These observations confirmed that the squirrels were going
after the sugar and not the water. On overcast days when temperatures remained below freezing, there was no sap run at all.
However, sugar concentrations at all of the sixty taps that I examined were above 55 percent. The lack of freshly running sap
to drink did not discourage the squirrels; for the first time I observed five feeding simultaneously. They were harvesting almost
pure sugar without having to contend with the large amounts of
water that may normally act as a deterrent. In retrospect, what I
found was not surprising. In the winter, the air is usually relatively
dry, because water condenses out of it at low temperatures. When
it warms up suddenly (as on sunny days when sap runs), the air
can hold more moisture, and evaporation is rapid. Thus, the ideal
conditions for a sap run coincide with the ideal conditions for
evaporation.

The red squirrels were doing more than opportunistically visiting tree wounds where there happened to be sugar. They were
methodically making the wounds themselves, which then served
as sugar taps. I saw no "natural" breakage wounds. Every one of
the hundreds of taps that I saw and that the squirrels visited were
made by them, and they were distinct and easy to identify.

The squirrels made their taps in a systematic, although seemingly casual, manner by pausing only for about a second or less
(while visiting nearby taps) to make a single bite into a branch

of a tree. These were not casual bites, however. As already mentioned, getting sap to run requires piercing the xylem below the bark. Each tap consisted of just a single two-millimeter puncture bite created by opposing pairs of teeth chiseling down in one clean sweep. The bite wounds usually left a narrow curl of bark where the teeth had penetrated. However, the squirrels made no attempt to remove anything with a bite; their tap making is not incidental to feeding on bark. Furthermore, the squirrels always moved on almost instantly after making a bite, not waiting for any immediate reward. Taps were revisited only hours or days after they were made. I found identical bite marks in sugar maple saplings at nineteen out of thirty-two other sites that I surveyed in Maine and Vermont.

The squirrels were highly selective in the trees they chose to tap. On January 28, a sample of fifteen young sugar maple trees in the clearing around my cabin revealed a total of 158 bite marks, while seventy-three other trees (twenty-five red maple, twenty white birch, twenty poplar, eight apple) showed no taps at all. When I resurveyed the trees one month later, the number of taps per sugar maple tree had tripled, but the non-maple trees remained unbitten. No new taps were made during the summer. But tapping was resumed immediately on two warm days following cold nights in late November.

I was surprised that the squirrels were able to distinguish between the red and sugar maple trees (a task that is daunting to most college students enrolled in my winter ecology course). But I suspect the squirrels may have been doing their tree taxonomy not so much on the basis of bud or bark morphology, but in part on a chemical basis. Squirrels are renowned for their ability to detect food by scent.

The squirrels always made their taps immediately *after* feeding.

Hence, if a previous wound yielded sugar, then that tree would soon have a second wound, creating a positive feedback loop that increased the number of taps on trees with high sugar concentration. I never found more than 6 taps on a single red maple, whereas one small sugar maple tree eventually had 102 taps.

Individual maple trees vary considerably in the amount and concentration of the sap they produce. For example, trees with narrow crowns in the deep woods produce much less sap than vigorously growing trees in open areas, such as those near my cabin. This may explain why the squirrels were apparently coming out of the nearby coniferous forests to work the sugar bush near the cabin.

As Lucia Jacobs has shown (see "Cache Economy of the Gray Squirrel," *Natural History*, October 1989), gray squirrels have a good memory and cache food to tide themselves over until spring. Red squirrels also cache and undoubtedly have good site memory. Indeed, my impression was that some squirrels (especially my tame ones near the cabin) visited a fairly regular "tap line" of trees. This impression gains support from the patterns of tracks on the snow. After one light overnight dusting of about a half inch on already deep, crusted snow, I followed the tracks leading to and from individual trees in my sugaring grove in order to find out which tees were most often visited. I conducted my surveys from 10 to 11 a.m., shortly after the animals had returned to the forest after their early morning sugar snack (many returned again in late afternoon). Written on the snow was the record of their choices. Of 93 sugar maple trees with taps, 74 had been visited, while none of the 15 untapped sugar maples had attracted squirrels. Of the 113 other untapped trees, only 7 had been climbed. The squirrels were specifically visiting those sugar maple trees with previously made sugar-yielding taps.

The amount of sugar per tap varies enormously over a matter of hours. However, on average, I measured 81 milligrams of sugar per tap. At 3.7 calories per milligram of sugar, a squirrel could potentially consume 300 calories per tap. Although the squirrel can collect this sugar in a minute or less, this amount is still not likely to be a major portion of the daily energy budget of about 117,000 calories for an adult male. Clearly the animals cannot rely on sugar treats as a steady diet; there are often many weeks in the winter when no sap flows at all, and sugar maples are not always available in habitats where the squirrels rely on the seeds of conifers for winter survival.

Although tapping probably satisfies only a small proportion of the squirrels' total energy budget, it may be the major food supply of some other members of the biological community. Wherever the sugar maple tree grows in North America, an assemblage of a dozen to about fifty species of winter-active moths, the Cuculiinae, are also found. These moths are endothermic, or warm-blooded, when active. Because of their high metabolism, the moths require large amounts of food energy. While most moths and butterflies feed on nectar, the source of these winter moths' energy supplies was previously unknown. For my studies of these moths, I needed a steady source of them and got them in large numbers routinely by smearing diluted maple syrup onto trees. If the moths feed on the maple syrup that is provided by squirrels, then their ability to function in winter is partly explained.

Having learned that red squirrels are accomplished harvesters of maple sugar for food makes me wonder how humans learned that a nearly tasteless, watery liquid found in maple trees can be made into a delicious food. I'm willing to entertain the thought that the red squirrel might have shown us.

Hibernation, Insulation, and Caffeination

New York Times, January 31, 2004

AN EMERITUS PROFESSOR ROLLING NAKED IN THE SNOW AT minus 20 degrees F and yelling like a banshee is either exhibiting an amazing remission from seasonal affective disorder or he is performing a slight (okay, a not-so-slight) act of braggadocio. In any case, I jumped right back into the sauna after twenty seconds, having briefly experienced an altered state of mind.

This was during my annual weeklong session on winter ecology, with a dozen biology students at my log cabin in the woods of western Maine. The idea is to stop just reading about nature and also start experiencing it; it is impossible to teach even the brightest scholars how coffee tastes unless you let them drink it. We had chosen mid-January for our winter tasting. We picked a good time: there was snow aplenty and temperatures were appropriate. And by the way, everyone survived, every single one.

The difference between just barely surviving the cold for a half minute and living through the whole winter outdoors is, of course, not trivial. Animals can show us how they manage, and their ways are stunningly diverse. From personal experience as a normal guy, I can vouch for the main ingredients needed for human survival: insulation, granola bars, and coffee (more on that later). Most people in this environment do not suffer from a calorie or a beverage deficit; we're seldom totally out of reach of a store.

But I'm not so sanguine about that first ingredient, insulation. The key is multiple layers or a thick layer of tightly sealed air. My L. L. Bean gear is usually adequate, but, as I learned empirically, that depends on where you are. Some years ago I was up north in Inuit country, in a little village full of dogs, where forty-pound "sausages" of walrus blubber were buried nearby under the tundra to ferment slowly on the permafrost. I saw some men loading up a sled with enough fuel canisters for their Yamaha snowmobiles to drive at least once around the North Pole; I asked to get on. "No way," was the answer, "unless you get rid of those white man's clothes."

I purchased a pair of sealskin gloves that reached up to my elbows, and a beautiful handmade parka of raw caribou hides, trimmed with wolf fur, that hung down to my knees. The fellows lent me sealskin boots and caribou pants, and I was set. I looked like the Yeti. And I felt like a king. I stayed almost warm as we rode some sixty miles on a minus-40-degree night; by daylight we arrived at a char-fishing and wolf- and caribou-hunting camp, where the char were piled up like pulpwood and skinned animal carcasses were strewn around. The lesson: in the far north, if you want to be up and about with the warm-blooded animals, you've got to dress like them.

Most of the mammals in the north change into a denser and deeper winter coat by late fall. Their signal fur-coat change is the "photoperiod" — the relative hours of daylight and dark. Man, a primate from the tropics, survives by taking his coat from the mammals. Our recently invented substitutes are a serviceable but pale imitation.

Birds' insulation is, per weight, even better. The chickadees get up on even the coldest morning at first dawn to search for food. Their body core temperatures are slightly higher than ours, and their insulating layer of feathers is less than an inch thick. Heat loss through the feathers is reduced by raising them, which is why many small birds look rounder and fatter as the winter drags on, even as they lose weight overnight (but regain it the next day).

Fluffing out to retard heat loss serves little purpose without constant heat production. That takes fueling with food, and the fuel costs rise sharply in winter, often just as the fuel supplies start to dwindle. That is why, like us, many other winter animals reduce their fuel costs by at times turning down their thermostat, huddling, and seeking shelter.

Northern flying squirrels bivouac in snug nests made of shredded cedar and birch bark, and may huddle together in same-sex groups of up to ten or more. In contrast, chipmunks gather food stores by fall and feed on them in their subterranean dens. They then may enter light torpor, especially when the nuts run out. Woodchucks store their energy in fat on their bodies and hibernate deeply all winter. The many without those energy-saving tricks or access to enough food are forced to migrate.

In looking at what different animals do to survive in the winter, one sees different but consistent patterns that solve the same problem. The fascinating part is to see how all of these solutions are fine-tuned to specific circumstances.

My Winter Ecology students prepared themselves for the week by bringing a large supply of food. With pleasure, I surveyed a mound of cheese from Vermont, fruit from Florida, raisins and nuts from California, flour and oats from the Midwest, chocolate made of cocoa, sugar, and milk all from I know not where. On any walk into the woods we were laden with munchies because we never found anything to eat along the way. We would not have survived, even if we had spears and bows to procure lunch.

As a teenager, I had the romantic notion of staying in these woods for a year and "living off the land" like an aboriginal hunter. But since then I've sat up in a tree for hours, for days, hoping for a glimpse of a deer — long enough to realize that this activity, subsidized by imported calories, would cost more than it could bring back. My shivering was quickly burning off the calories of my candy bars, dissipating them into the icy void.

I could not help but contemplate the strategy that the Ice Age Neanderthals might have used in the forests of central Europe, where they did not have access to the plenitude of the seacoast, yet survived for thousands of years. Might they have hibernated, like bears? Bears have the ability to gorge and fatten up when food is abundant and then remain inactive for long periods — and some of us seem pre-adapted along those lines. I wonder what they thought of our species when it arrived, and vice versa.

In the winter, I usually feel myself getting drowsy near 4:30 p.m. when it starts to get dark, and I'm not awake until the morning light. An artificial light might keep me up a little longer, but not much. I'm able to get by with remarkably few hours of waking time, but I'm certain they could be extended by light at one end, and the promise of a cup of coffee at the other.

So perhaps I am a victim of seasonal affective disorder, with its slowness and melancholy. By some it is considered a pathological condition, but I wonder. I'm now inclined to think it's *not* a disease. I think it may be a vestigial remnant of an adaptive hibernation response. If you live in the woods, where the lights stay dim and the cabin cold, a naked romp in the snow after a hot sauna may be just the right winter survival trick to shock you back to life.

Cohabiting with Elephants: A Browsing Relationship

Natural History, May 2017

I WAS WEANED ON THE CONCEPT OF AN ECOLOGICAL BALANCE in nature, built on an intricate web of relationships among plants, herbivores, predators, and other life forms, where the fate of one can have a domino effect on the others.

Last fall, I was near the equator in the Moremi Game Reserve on Botswana's Okavango Delta, one of the most pristine wildernesses on earth, containing perhaps a representative set of Pleistocene fauna. Maintenance of this vast wilderness is a national mission: no hunting, logging, herding, or industrial agriculture are allowed. I arrived at the beginning of the rainy season, and some of the trees were starting to break bud. However, I found myself in what looked like a tree-killing zone. Large trees had been toppled — some freshly felled, others moldering back into the ground. If I had witnessed this scene at home, I would have guessed the cause was a weather event — wind shear, hurricane, ice storm — or perhaps clear-cut logging. In this virgin wilderness there was something else surprising — something violating another of my

cherished ecological concepts. Throughout the devastated landscape were large patches of low trees of nearly a single species: the
mopane tree, *Colophospermum mopane*. Likewise, many, if not
most, of the large destroyed trees were also mopane.

Tree species diversity is notoriously high in the tropics and declines steadily moving away from the equator (for a number of
possible reasons). This diversity maintains conditions that allow
multiple animal species to survive, as one species depends for its
survival on the others. Here, in fauna-rich Botswana, there *should*
be many species of trees. Some areas had a density of trees, yet
these mopane woodlands cover vast expanses of northern parts
of the Republic of South Africa, Botswana, Malawi, Zambia, Zimbabwe, Namibia, Angola, and the Republic of the Congo. Why do
these areas have such low tree-diversity forests when Africa, especially southern Africa, has extraordinarily high plant and animal
species diversity? Why were there so few tree species in Botswana's Okavango Delta, a seasonally hot area with plenty of water
readily available close to the ground surface?

Variations in the forms of the mopane tree may be a clue. Mo-
panes were growing in patches of three main forms. The trees
were huge in semi-open forest, along with other tall trees such
as acacias, fever trees, rain trees, and leadwood trees. There, they
reached roughly thirty meters in height. In other patches, they
were only two to three meters tall and spread uniformly in all directions like huge unkempt grape arbors. In their third form, they
were near ten to fifteen meters tall, and also spread evenly and
widely. Such varied forms and distribution are not indicative of
a species that fits into a well-established ever-constant niche created by or adapted to others, but rather of one responding possibly
in a variety of ways to episodic predation pressures or episodic
weather events.

A large species of emperor moth, *Gonimbrasia belina,* lays its egg clusters primarily on mopane leaves, which are the prime diet of the larvae in all their stages of development. The trees, however, easily survive damage from "mopane worms," as they are commonly known. Something large and more destructive was laying waste to the trees. Elephants and long-term drought were the obvious suspects.

During my visit, elephants were beginning to return to the bush, feeding on freshly leafed-out mopane. They had been concentrated for months during the dry season near the waters of the Khwai River. We saw forty-nine elephants on one day's travel. During the height of the wet season, we could expect to see six to eight hundred per day, according to our guide, depending, no doubt, on geographic cycles of drought.

As it turns out, elephants, as well as mopane worms, goats, cattle, kudu, and impala, all relish mopane leaves because of their high nitrogen content — typical also to other members of the pea family — and, possibly, because of the water content. Elephants, however, can reach into the tops of young trees and browse the lower branches of even large trees. Their browsing, depending on when it occurs, can sculpt the trees' form. In the areas where mopane trees were uniformly two to three meters tall, each tree had become multi-stemmed, as it regrew in several directions from the bottom, presumably after the tops and branches had been stripped off. In patches where the trees were tall, they had no branches within six meters of the ground, because those branches had been within reach of the elephants. When these trees were young, they had escaped elephant browsing, most likely because elephants were then absent. Once these trees had achieved sufficient height, despite elephants clearing lower branches, they had concentrated their growth at their tops. Some became formed like massive umbrellas. Intermediate-sized trees, whose upper branches were out of reach, had been knocked down by elephants. Weighing three to six tons each, elephants found few trees to be a challenge. The largest trees remained standing a much longer time, and were left as the elephants' last pick, some eventually being debarked up to several meters by tusks, rather than getting pushed over. Debarked trees eventually weaken, die, and remain standing as dry skeletons. But mopane trees have a unique physiology that adds another dimension to this scenario.

Elephants, or a prolonged drought, could potentially eliminate all trees in an area. Afterward, there would have been regrowth for the mopane as formerly decimated areas were recolonized. When elephants returned, they could have favored certain species and eventually eliminated them locally. As we approached the town of Maun — the gateway to the Okavango Delta — almost all the small acacia trees were heavily browsed, and many had been nearly destroyed. But in the town, where there are few or no elephants, large acacia trees were still intact. If people were to be suddenly gone, elephants would move in, attracted by the acacia, their favorite browse, and they would remove the trees' lower branches. The trees' growth would then shift to the tops, and an open woodland of tall umbrella-like trees would result. Many would then get knocked down, and the forest would be destroyed. Another would replace it, provided the tree browsers were absent for a sufficient time. The point in time when the browsers returned would dictate the shape of the trees.

The mopane has also been under the strong selective pressure of elephant grazing. The two have likely had a history of millions of years of coevolution. However, this tree's apparent weakness of being fodder for elephants may have turned into an advantage, much as savanna grasses have effectively evolved a dependency on browsers such as wildebeests. Most tree species that are knocked down soon die, but young intermediate-sized mopane trees that are pushed over by elephants, and browsed upon, still retain some root in the ground. These trees, unlike most others, not only can revive, but also can put down many more roots along the whole length of their fallen trunks. New branches sprout from the still-living tree trunk, and they grow upward to become new vertical trunks, and hence several trees sprout from what had been one. Similarly, where elephants had browsed younger mopane trees, these trees had generated new branches. Seed dispersal occurs from eating the fruit, and thus elephants — by their bruising treatment of this tree — help propagate it. In the first week of December, when I was visiting the area, I tracked new twigs that grew a foot long. Trees still had six to seven more months of growing time. With such growth, it is no wonder that these trees survive, and thrive. The trees' varied forms in relatively uniform patches attest to periodic absences of elephants in the past, which allowed for sustained growth to reach different stages before massive browsing recurred.

Mopane trees are not the only beneficiaries of cohabitating with elephants. When elephants clear ground by knocking over or killing many trees but leaving the largest specimens, they create a parklike, albeit untidy, environment. Sunlight reaches the ground and grasses sprout. Hippos, traveling in and out of nearby rivers to browse on the grass, create channels for spreading water. At the beginning of the wet season, I saw shoots of grass, herbs, and tree seedlings emerging from the ground. Impala were there in herds, with their fresh and frisky fawns. Wild dogs and leopards were sure to follow. All of the grazers of the grassy plain and the biota in the bush and in woodlands may owe their debt of existence to elephants. I had not appreciated the factor of time and ecological succession until seeing this. Elephants, because they are large and powerful and because they travel huge distances, blur the ecological boundaries of time and place, which define much of the African landscape, in the long run.

The Hunt: A Matter of Perspective

Natural History, March 2017

AT DAWN IN THE OKAVANGO DELTA, A BIRD CHORUS WAS just starting up. We were clustered around a smoldering campfire in an unfenced clearing under tall leadwood trees in the Moremi Game Reserve. Ras Munduu, our Botswanan safari leader and guide, casually walked to the edge of our clearing and ran back shouting, "Quick, quick, get in the truck!" Having heard hyenas, hippos, and lions in the night, our party of four scrambled to jump in behind him. "Dogs!" he said.

After a frenetic ten-minute ride, we found ourselves in a pastoral setting among seventeen African wild dogs (*Lycaon pictus*). They were lolling about in the dry grass on the remains of an old termite mound. A thin mist lay over the green channel of the nearby Khwai River. Hippos had returned from their nocturnal roaming. In anticipation of another hundred-degree day, they were submerged in the river while crocodiles basked beside it. Elephants were coming to drink, and more than two hundred Cape buffalo, which had arrived in the night, were now accompanied by cattle egrets and oxpeckers. We heard the deep but faint roar of a lion in the distance. The dogs were at ease, playing and looking like a passel of lean painted pooches, each blotched in a unique pattern of black, yellow, or chocolate, and each distinguished by its behavior.

African Cape buffalo.

As the dogs noodled about next to our open-sided Land Cruiser, they took no visible notice of us, making us feel as if we were wearing an invisibility cloak. We were strongly admonished, however, not to reach or lean out, or talk. The vehicle seemed to be a mutually accepted safe zone with prescribed rules of engagement between us and the wildlife.

One of the dogs suddenly stood stock-still, pricked up its large ears, and gazed into the distance. The others did likewise, as did we. From our position we saw only a vast expanse of low, elephant-browsed mopane trees. Scattered rain trees and fever trees also had their limbs browsed bare, up to a height of twenty feet, by elephants and giraffe. The dog that had alerted the pack suddenly bounded off. The rest followed but only in the same general direction; they spread out. A hunt was on. We took off after them. "They can run like this forever," Ras said. While "forever" was hyperbole, the day was still cool, and the dogs and their intended prey would not easily overheat and slow down.

After a several-minute wild ride following the dogs, we saw zebras. One of the dogs veered off and approached the herd. Rather than running, the zebras formed a circle around a young colt. One of the zebras of the group stepped forward. The dog backed down from the challenge and rejoined the others. After a few more minutes, we saw impala, small, graceful antelope, that were running faster than the dogs. Yet in less than ten minutes, we heard, from back in a large thicket, the telltale bleating of a kill in progress. Hours after birth, baby impala are agile, fast runners, but these young are not fast enough to outrun a pack of dogs. Their mothers had hidden them in the bush and then run off, acting as decoys. The fawns, however, must have been flushed. Dogs emerged from the bush, carrying the remains of three fawns, and some were having tugs of war over the parts. Others were lying about, tearing and chewing the meat. The dogs had been silent throughout the hunt, but now some made high-pitched chittering noises as they approached those that had already feasted, begging them to share by regurgitating what they had just hastily ingested.

The dogs were a team. It takes a group to make a successful hunt — prey that escapes one dog may inadvertently run into another — but the group must be small enough for all to share the quarry. As with wolves, only one pair in the pack breeds. Breeding privilege is based on merit, which in wolves and in African wild dogs depends on status or strengths, which subsume health and heredity. Division of labor in reproduction, as in the hunt, permits some members to tend a den of young pups while others hunt.

Before we had witnessed the hunt, we had felt emotionally moved by the beauty and grace of impala and their fawns, the most endearing, slender-legged, joyfully prancing creatures imaginable. It is hard not to empathize with them. Yet we were not entirely neutral in the outcome of the chase. We became transfixed by the dogs and transferred our allegiance to them. As we saw their strategies unfold, we felt participation; we were pseudo-predators, stepping back into the mindset of the Pleistocene hominids who once hunted here. They probably had a social system similar to the dogs'. They ate meat. Being bipedal, they were good runners. And they would have shared the spoils of the hunt by bringing it back to a home, or a lair. We were drawn by the same instincts, except our spoils were the images and stories we hoped to capture and bring home to savor and to share.

From small to large, there were predators everywhere in the Botswanan game reserve, but we had so far — despite driving and exploring ten hours per day for three days — not sighted lions, although every night, when sounds carry far in the cooler moisture-saturated air, we had heard rumbles of what seemed like distant thunder, except they were pulsed in a rhythm. On our fourth night of hearing these distant rumbles, Ras declared that there were lions six to seven kilometers away. The next morning at 5 a.m., when we heard the sound again, Ras started the engine of the Land Cruiser and called out, "Let's go!" Tourist talk to whip up enthusiasm, I thought. No way could anyone pinpoint the location of a specific animal in this vast, 4,870-square-kilometer tract of pristine wilderness. But we loaded up and tore off on another wild hunt. Like the first, it promised excitement, no matter what we might see, merely due to the elements of speed, expectations, possible discoveries, surprises, and companionship of the like-minded.

Our journey took us down bumpy and curvy single-lane sand paths through mixed woodland and grasslands. The first rains had begun to sprout shoots of grass on the tawny dry ground. The landscape was flat to our eyes, but to Botswanans there are elevated islands among the various lagoons of the Khwai River, where massive trees grow. Eons ago, winds brought white sand and sculpted the islands. They were made suitable for life by the water that floods them after heavy rains flow south from Angola during January and February. Hippos created channels that helped distribute the water, and termites built mounds twenty feet high on which the trees grow.

After about a half-hour, we stopped to photograph a giraffe. Like all animals here in the reserve, it had no fear of us in a vehicle. At first we heard only birdsong; then we heard a series of deep rumbles. We were close to the lions. In less than ten minutes, ahead of us on the flat top of an abandoned termite mound, lay a mature male with a shaggy brown mane and a grizzled face, staring off into the distance as we drove within fifteen feet of him. He was so close, we could see his thin body hair speckled with flies. None of us could avert our eyes from him, but he did not even bother to turn his head to look at us. Instead, his gaze reached into the distance. It was minutes before he slowly turned our way and we could look into his bright yellow eyes. He yawned and revealed a massive maw and an impressive set of teeth, then turned his head back and resumed semi-somnolence. A younger male, his partner, lay about two hundred meters distant, similarly at ease. Male lions often pair up with another male, usually a littermate, to overpower males holding prides.

These two lions were roaring to proclaim their territory and discourage challengers. Their pride of females, according to Ras, would be in the vicinity, or at least within hearing distance, or several kilometers. As we watched for some ten or more minutes, the older lion started to rouse himself, making a few soft rumbles. His belly then heaved and the rumbles became louder and louder, as he held his head higher and higher. We were stunned by the volume heard at such close proximity. We stayed a half-hour to watch this fully wild animal, which had no more regard for us than he had for a weaverbird or a glossy starling. Ras speculated that he and his younger partner were gearing up for a fight to defend their territory and pride. A single lion would have no chance against this reigning pair. Their challengers, however, might be a pair of five-year-old brothers who live in the same area and who were now coming of age. Ras thought they would be well matched against this pair, which had so far maintained dominance for three or four years. If the challenging pair succeeded, they would kill all the cubs in the defending pair's pride, which would bring the females into heat.

Females are complicit in these contests. To ensure their cubs' survival, they promote challenges that test dominance. But how can females decide with whom they have the best future? They fake being in heat, which induces mating by the newcomers, which in turn leads to fights. For the mothers, a victory by the younger challengers usually means greater long-term security.

· · ·

Our hunt for the top predator in the Moremi Game Reserve was successful, with images and stories as trophies. We moved on to find smaller game. After an hour of driving, we stopped to photograph a carmine bee-eater. Its gorgeous red and blue coloring was striking. Ras drove us to its source — a breeding colony of hundreds. These birds normally make nesting burrows on high riverbanks. But there are no riverbanks on the Okavango Delta, and for this colony, the birds' hundreds of burrows were on a table-flat plain. A kite showed up amid the fluttering of birds, perhaps hunting for a young or injured baby. A bateleur eagle soared overhead.

As we were leaving the birds, driving past a bushy low acacia bush, we spied two male lions lying side by side in its shade. Ras declared they were the five-year-old littermates, the possible challengers to the pair of lions we had just left.

We watched this pair as long as we had watched the first, but they made no sound. Admiring them from up close, we noted that the one to the left kept looking up into the sky. Ras said, "Lions are lazy. He is observing vultures — to find out where to find a fresh kill." A bateleur eagle was also flying, but the lion watched only the spot in the sky in the other direction. Eventually, we saw one, then two, vultures soaring. They were gradually coming lower. The lion maintained his rapt attention, eyes up and locked on. The other remained stretched out flat, perhaps asleep. The first got up, and with slow measured steps walked within several feet of our vehicle, then continued in a beeline toward where the vultures had just come down. He sauntered on, without a single glance back. Eventually, the second righted his front end and watched his brother with apparent rising interest.

At that point we decided to follow the leading lion. We drove ahead of him and then circled around and got into position among some trees, hoping to intercept him. Soon enough, he appeared and broke into a steady trot. He kept on through tall grasses and then climbed onto a termite mound; we then parked nearby. Within a minute, the second lion appeared, also trotting. He joined his brother, and the two stayed side by side, watching the vultures, several of which had by now landed in treetops. "We've got to connect the dots," Ras said, and speculated that the vultures were not yet on the ground because the animal that made the kill — likely, a leopard or a cheetah — was still nearby. The lions were waiting for it to leave, which might take a day or more, so we left without seeing the end of the drama.

Several days later, having left behind the invisibility cloak of the Land Cruiser, I was forty thousand feet above the ground, traveling at around six hundred miles per hour. The sixteen-hour flight gave me time to reflect on the wonder of having seen and experienced, as near as is possible, the Pleistocene environment of our ancestors two to four million years ago. The tracks Lucy left in the stone at Laetoli about four million years ago took on new meaning. A similar assembly of animals would have roamed then, doing what these do now. *Australopithecus* (or whatever ape-man came after) would have had to be localized to where there was a reliable source of water. Small isolated populations can generate rapid evolution. The dangers meant deaths were frequent, selection strong. Meat was plentiful, especially concentrated near water. If lions could locate hyena, leopard, and dog kills, so could our forebears. They too could have followed the vultures, but on foot. They would have waited until the heat of the day had produced the thermals on which birds ride as they patrol the ground and the predators were resting lazily in the shade, not eager to travel. Hominids had the capacity to tolerate the heat through sweating as well as a low profile to the sun, a sun shield of hair and melanin. Most significant, allowing them to be there at all, they had grasping forelimbs. They had hands free to wield weapons — rocks, sticks, and clubs — and the collective will to use them. Soon enough, they became selective in what they held, and some started to alter what they held into tools and weapons.

Endurance Predator

Outside, September 2000

I WAS STANDING IN AN ANCIENT LANDSCAPE IN EAST AFRICA. All around me white and yellow flowering acacia trees were abuzz with bees, wasps, and colorful cetoniid beetles. Baboons and impala roamed in the miombe bush. Herds of wildebeests and zebras thundered by daily. In the distance, elephants and rhinoceroses lumbered over the rolling hills. Caught up in searching for dung beetles for the study I had come for, I happened to peek under an auspicious rock overhang and was taken aback by what I saw.

Painted on the wall was a succession of sticklike human figures, clearly in full running stride, all clutching delicate bows, quivers, and arrows and running in one direction, left to right, across the rock canvas. This was a two- or three-thousand-year-old pictograph, with nothing particularly extraordinary about it — until I noticed something that sent my mind reeling: the figure leading the procession had its hands thrust upward in what seemed to me to be the universal sign of athletic victory, a gesture reflexive in runners who have fought hard and then feel the exhilaration of triumph.

This happened years ago, in Zimbabwe's Matobo National Park (formerly Matopos Park), but it remains for me an enduring reminder that the roots of our biology, during the Pleistocene, relate to our heritage as endurance predators.

Looking at that African rock painting made me feel I was witness to a kindred spirit, a man who had long ago vanished yet whom I understood as if we'd talked just a moment earlier. I was not only in the same environment and of the same mind as the unknown Bushman, but I was also in the place that most likely produced our common ancestors. The artist had been here hundreds of generations before me, but that was only the blink of an eye compared to the eons that have elapsed since a bipedal intermediate between our apelike and recognizably human ancestors left the safety of the forest for the savanna some four million years ago.

It wasn't an easy transition. Indeed, it had fateful physiological and psychological consequences that are still deeply embedded in our bodies and our psyches. Standing before that long-lost victor in the struggle to survive, I was reminded of what I was, still am, and perhaps what we will forever be as long as we are human.

We were all runners once. Although some of us forget that primal fact — because the selective pressures for the running hunt have long since been extinguished. But comparative biology teaches us that life on the plains generates arms races between predators and prey — and our ancestors definitely weren't into unilateral disarmament. Meat was abundant for those who could catch it or wrest it from the competition, that is, leopards and lions, not to mention hyenas, jackals, and vultures. Because we primates weren't superb sprinters, we needed alternatives to sheer speed in those wide-open spaces in order to eat. So like our hominid ancestors, we traveled in groups, racing overland to fresh-killed carcasses and chasing off scavengers. These skirmishes, as

well as infighting within our own species — that is, our first true
competitors — became the bridge to hunting live prey. The faster
and farther you could run, the more valuable you became in the
new social groups based on the hunt.

In 1961 I spent a year collecting birds in Africa for Yale's Pea-
body Museum, and I experienced, I think, what ancient hunters
were up against. I'll never forget my feelings of dreary claustro-
phobia during the months we spent in dense, dripping mountain
forests, nor, alternatively, the feeling of glorious exhilaration out
on the open steppes. To catch even small birds, I had to wander ex-
tensively, half of each day, just as our ancestors must have done. By
about two to three million years ago, they had a leg and foot structure almost identical to our own, and it's reasonable to assume
that they walked and ran like we do. While other predators rested,
I was able to continue, albeit slowly, because we humans have one
major physical advantage: we can sweat, copiously, which allows
us to manage our internal temperature, which in turn extends our
endurance. Few animals living in a hot and dry environment and
without ready access to water can afford such a mechanism of
profligate water use. Through the ages and across the continents
there are examples of men actually chasing down beasts that are
much faster. In fact, there are modern reports of the Paiute and
Navajo of North America hunting pronghorn antelope on foot by
patiently running down a stray until it drops in its tracks from
exhaustion and then reverently suffocating the animal by hand. In
Africa, the San (Bushmen) chase down giraffe and large antelope
such as kudu, which because of their large size have a problem
getting rid of internally generated heat since they must be sparing
with water. The trick to running them down is to hunt in the heat
of the day, a time when the great predators rest in the shade.

Now we chase one another rather than kudu or other antelope, woolly mammoths, or deer. But the basic body movements required for hunting and for warfare — throwing, running, jumping — have become ritualized in track and field events, which are still the heart and soul, if not the very essence, of the Olympics. The games are simply mock wars waged in the spirit of camaraderie, though they retain the intensity of their origins. The difference is that in a contest with prey there is always an endpoint: we get it, or it gets away. In our races against one another, in our constant striving to better our achievements and set new records, there is no apparent end. Where, then, are the limits? World and Olympic records have been kept for more than a century, but over that span there never has been a year in which records have not been broken. Performances that were world-class only fifty years ago are almost routine now. Again and again, feats thought physiologically impossible have been surpassed. In 1954, Roger Bannister ran the mile in 3:59.40 to break the four-minute barrier, which at that time stunned the world. But within six weeks even that improbable mark fell, a feat that has since become almost routine. Fast-forward to 1999, and the Moroccan Hicham El Guerrouj lowered the record to 3:43.13.

So it goes: in the Mexico City Olympics of 1968, Bob Beamon shattered Ralph Boston's long-jump world record of twenty-seven feet, four and one-quarter inches with a jump of twenty-nine feet, two and a half inches. For nearly twenty-three years Beamon's record was considered to be beyond unbreakable, until the 1991 World Championships in Tokyo, where Carl Lewis came within one inch of it and Mike Powell actually beat it by two inches at the same meet.

The first modern record for the hundred-meter dash was 11 seconds, set by Great Britain's William MacLaren in 1867. It got chipped away over the next several decades until the American

Charles Paddock dropped it to 10.2 seconds in 1921. His time didn't see a major improvement until 1956, when his countryman Willie Williams ran a 10.1. Then, last year, the U.S. sprinter Maurice Greene set a world record of 9.79.

The steady improvement in records of all sporting events may, at first glance, look like biological evolution, but this could not be further from the truth. Evolution might still have played a role shaping us back in the ice ages, when we were fragmented into small isolated populations, regularly dropping dead not just due to athletic deficiencies but also many forms of bad luck. No more. Living as we now do, in large, increasingly homogenized populations, any mutations that might crop up and that could be of value for athletic performance would quickly be diffused in the gene pool since selection for it stopped long ago.

That's not to say changes can't happen. Could a species stuck with our bipedal design evolve and someday run as fast as ostriches? Maybe we're still so unspecialized for the task of running that selective breeding could accomplish this. But even if we attempted that unthinkable experiment — if we bred humans like, say, racehorses, along lines of pedigree — the project would probably have to continue uninterrupted for hundreds or thousands of years. We have no idea what makes a Secretariat different from an also-ran, but if we want to beat a Secretariat, we begin with Secretariat genes. Still, if we did create human thoroughbreds, there's good reason to believe the physical "improvement" would eventually stop; despite selective breeding, thoroughbreds haven't gotten any faster over the past hundred years. Why should it be any different with us?

Genetically we're pretty much the same as we've been for hundreds of thousands of years; the basic changes for running, throwing, jumping, and the like were made long ago, and the trajectory, and eventual endpoint, were determined then as well. Physiologically speaking with respect to running, on average we may well be devolving, so to speak; if we picked one of our six billion brethren at random and had that person run against a fit-for-survival Pleistocene man or woman, there's a good chance we'd come out the loser.

Don't tell that to Michael Johnson. To understand performances like his, it's important to recognize that, in terms of genetics, training, and nutrition, a world-record performance is the far, far end of the normal distribution. Olympians don't represent typical physiology. Far from it. World-class athletes are generally off the scale according to every parameter one can think of — physiological systems for muscles, enzymes, hormones, bone structure, body build, motivation, and dedication. Moreover, all of these superlatives have been bolstered by the best knowledge and execution of diet, rest, training, and stress management. In an Olympic athlete, more and more we're looking at a freak, an elite specimen who is not like you or me and who is specialized to do one thing extremely well — necessarily at the expense of other things.

Each event has circumscribed specifications. For instance, the very best sprinters don't need much aerobic capacity because they rely on a preponderance of fast-twitch muscle fibers, which contract quickly and anaerobically, meaning they don't require oxygen to burn fuel. Those same athletes could not successfully run distance, because long-distance runners rely on a huge aerobic capacity and a larger percentage of slow-twitch fibers, which contract at a slower rate but can work for long periods, so long as they're being continually supplied with oxygen. These traits are largely inherited: if your muscles are made up of mostly slow-twitch fibers, you'll simply never be explosive. We might be able to do a lot to change the basic design we're born with, but not to the point of achieving a world-beating performance.

In the early days of Olympic and world competition, the athletes were probably closer in ability to the average population. Nevertheless, they came from a small pool out of the total population, and that pool came largely from the privileged class or those who, for one odd reason or another, decided to throw the javelin, long jump, sprint, or run the marathon. Such is not the case now. First, talent is actively solicited: individuals are identified, nurtured, and encouraged to pursue their dreams to the near-exclusion of more distracting concerns, like milking the cows or otherwise making a living. A second and perhaps much more significant phenomenon is that the pool from which the talented are selected has expanded dramatically. Since 1896, when the first modern Olympics were held, the world population has quadrupled. What's more, while Olympians were previously drawn only from Europe, Australia, and North America, now they also come from Asia, Africa, and South America. Statistically, by simply increasing the sample size, you increase the likelihood of having some individual runner who is faster than ever before in history (as well as one who is slower than ever before).

The only real evolution has been in realms not directly related to biology. The most obvious factor in athletic improvement has been better technology. Running shoes are infinitely better. Vaulting poles morphed from ash to bamboo to aluminum to fiberglass, nearly doubling the record heights in the event. And of course, swimsuits have undergone all manner of makeovers, from wool trunks and tops in the early twentieth century to skimpy Lycra numbers in the disco years to full-body suits debuting in Sydney called fastskins, which have a dimpled surface, much like a golf ball's, to reduce drag.

Accompanying the technological breakthroughs have been changes in technique, such as Dick Fosbury's now-standard backward flop over the high-jump bar and swimmer David Berkoff's dolphin kick in the backstroke. Training methods have also evolved. Germany's Woldemar Gerschler used interval training to help his protégé, Rudolf Harbig, nab the world record of 1:46.60 in the eight-hundred-meter run in 1939. Arthur Lydiard of New Zealand helped Peter Snell take Olympic gold in the same event in 1960 and 1964 by advocating long, slow running to build endurance, and brutal hill work to build strength. And Britain's Sebastian Coe, who in 1981 set an eight-hundred-meter world record that held for sixteen years, used weightlifting in addition to Gerschler's and Lydiard's methods.

Such a multitude of factors makes it nigh impossible to predict limits, but physical limits exist. In just one century the law of diminishing returns has already set in; in certain track events, decades pass in which records improve by no more than hundredths of a second. Take the two-hundred-meter run: in 1968, the world record stood at 19.83 seconds; in 1996 Michael Johnson lowered it to 19.32 seconds — about a half a second over twenty-eight years.

None of this is good news for the human spirit. We need to keep desire alive. We keep the faith that records will fall only to those who believe it is possible, that the heroes that achieved records did so through sheer guts and work. At our core, we are endurance predators driven by dreams, spurred on by the antelope that we can't see but know is out there, somewhere up ahead. To continue pushing, though, we must believe it's catchable — if only we apply ourselves.

Like the North American antelope's residual ability to outrun a cheetah — a cat that became extinct on the continent some ten thousand years ago — our abilities to run, throw, and jump are leftovers in our survival tool kit. As such, we use them in play because they are instinctually important to us. I'm not as athletically capable as an antelope or a bird or an Olympic athlete, but I enjoy my own capacities and I'm inspired to stretch them by comparing my abilities to what others can do. I'm humbled by what is routine to the songbird or sandpiper, awed by their ability to fly unbelievably long distances to and from specific pinpoints on the globe, such as some sandpiper's 11,680-kilometer flights nonstop from Alaska, across the Pacific Ocean, to New Zealand in 8.1 days, and then back home a few months later.

Some might argue that if I were a bird, I would not be able to enjoy my fantastic annual journeys, following the sun from perpetual daylight on the Arctic tundra to the pampas in Argentina and back again. But I think they are wrong. What makes the godwits and blackpoll warbler strike out south in the fall after a cold front is probably not fundamentally different from what motivates me to jog on a country road on a warm and sunny day. We're both responding to ancient urges. Proof that, in our case, it's impossible to extinguish our primal enthusiasm for the chase.

(Since I wrote a version of this piece for Outside *magazine, the use of performance-enhancing drugs by some athletes has come to light. My attempt here has been to refer only to performance in accordance with accepted rules and fair play.)*

STRATEGIES FOR LIFE

Synchronicity:
Amplifying the Signal

Natural History, September 2016

WAKING AT DAWN ONE SPRING MORNING, I HEARD A TURKEY gobble, loud and clear. It was close. Looking out the window, I saw two toms walking leisurely side by side. Their heads were held high, and every few steps they gobbled anew. One had fluffed up his back feathers. Each had the typical hanging throat tassel. One had white skin on the top of his bald head. In less than a minute both were directly below my window, where one suddenly launched into the full male display, with wings drooping and tail flared up into a huge fan. He assumed his dramatic display only between his gobble calls. When the toms got close, I could see their throats more clearly and noticed they were gobbling in perfect unison. I tried to see which one started the sound, but their throat movements were too perfectly synchronous for me to determine which began first.

A sleek female then came walking across the clearing, heading toward my bird feeder. She displayed no apparent attention to the toms as she casually walked past them about ten meters away. The toms stood still, fluffed out, and raised their heads high, displaying their bright, blood-engorged, flushed faces while their blue wattles slung down over their bills. After a while, the larger male with the bald white head again performed the tail-fan and wing-drag displays, but with the added flourish of a brief body quiver. He then began striding slowly, in a way that suggested he flowed rather than walked. The second male merely fluffed himself out.

The hen stopped feeding on the sunflower seeds after some minutes, lifted her head, and looked around. She then sauntered back across the clearing and into the woods. The two males stood tall and watched all the while until she was almost out of sight, and then they began following her in silence. The smaller male led, as the larger and more dominant one walked behind, occasionally fluffing and flaring his tail. It seemed as though the two males were cooperating in an attempted seduction. I would have liked to know the rest of the story, but there was nothing more to see, and the event soon seemed like a wonder from the past.

A single female continued to come to the feeder for the next week. About two weeks later, I saw a female coming, but this time a huge tom was stalking her from about twenty meters behind. His tassel was so long it dragged on the ground, and the top of his head was not just pale, but a chalky white. His face around the eyes was a brilliant blue. Fleshy, flabby bright-crimson skin was hanging on his neck. His green-copper shimmering back, light-tan wings, and earthen-brown tail made quite a show. Every few seconds he performed his spectacular fluffing, tail-fanning display. The female could not help but know he was behind her. He perhaps didn't need to gobble, so he stayed silent. She didn't show a hint of noticing him. He, on the other hand, remained focused on her as she pecked at the ground before wandering off. The following spring, I observed another single tom stalking a hen, staying about twenty meters behind her and occasionally displaying. She never glanced back, either.

Over several spring seasons, toms came regularly to our feeder. They came in ones, twos, and threes. They fed and left without fuss. Some gobbled regularly, but usually stayed out of sight in the woods surrounding the clearing. I seldom saw displays, and no interactions with hens except once, when two toms again showed interest in one hen. She fluttered up at one point to stay a few feet ahead of them, as they followed her. The toms gobbled only twice, and made a brief tail-fan display before they disappeared into the woods. The next day a group of four toms sauntered by with no hens in sight. None gobbled, and none made any display.

I considered the two synchronous male turkeys as an anomalous event, and probably would not have taken another look if one of them had pushed or chased the other away, as that is expected. All spring long, all other male woodland birds signal and maintain their individual identities. A lone woodcock sky-dances over the clearing every night. A grouse drums in a part of the woods, causing a second to stay away. Male woodpeckers tap out a beat, as another answers from an adjacent territory. Every warbler species has its own song with which it advertises itself in order to maintain an exclusive territory.

Synchronicity of animal vocalizations, however, is not unusual at our doorstep in the Maine woods. In spring, wood frogs create bedlam in our vernal pool. This year, the pool contained approximately three hundred egg masses, which means about three hundred females had arrived at the pool within several days — right after the ice melted — and likely a similar number of males came too. The males were often spread over the pool surface, about ten centimeters apart, and the sound waves of their calling creates ripple rings around them. At times, they were silent. And then one frog would start up, and in a minute or so the mayhem resumed as one frog after another popped back up from hiding under dead leaves on the pool bottom and joined in. To test whether they synchronized their display, I recorded them and then played the recording back to them during periods of silence. Invariably, playback caused them to come to the surface and resume chorusing at the same time, though not all in unison.

Elsewhere, I've observed synchronicity of a different sort, by bullfrogs. In Vermont, at the edge of a large wetland on warm nights in July, bullfrogs *garumph*. Unlike other local frogs (including wood frogs), these bullfrogs do call in unison throughout the bog, but only for several seconds, followed by several seconds of silence, followed again by the same duration of loud *garumph*ing. This rhythmic pattern continues for hours, giving the impression that the whole wetland has a steady beat of its own. It is awe-inspiring, not only for its volume, but also for its unvarying regularity.

Synchronicity of vocalizations is not restricted to birds and amphibians. Throughout the winter in the north woods, coyotes perform nocturnal singing concerts. On a cold, still, and otherwise quiet night, a single coyote starts the program with a mournful howl, followed quickly by another coyote chiming in, and then high-pitched yipping and various other voices joining in to create a pleasing harmony. It goes on for a minute or so, trails off in a yip or two, and then there is again the stillness of the night. These concerts resemble the more deeply pitched and mournful yet powerful chorus of gray wolves. Similarly, domestic dogs will join in with howls upon hearing a passing siren, or if humans take the lead with a musical instrument such as a harmonica. The function of synchronous howls is not definitive: perhaps this synchronicity is for information transmission, emotional expression, or both.

Howling may establish or signal to others of pack solidarity, for any of a variety of evolutionary reasons, such as territoriality.

Mammals around the world are some of the noisiest species, and many of them synchronize their singing. Gibbons are considered the songbirds of the primate family. Some species sing solo, having likely evolved from ancestors whose males and females had different songs but produced duets. The harmonized duets of a male and female pair, joined by their offspring, mark the boundaries of their territory. Siamang gibbons can be heard at distances of up to two miles through dense forest. They are considered the loudest land mammals on earth. Other noisy primates that come to mind are howler monkeys in Central America, colobus monkeys in Africa, and the indri of Madagascar. The latter live in small social groups that sing together several times a day. The synchronized vocalizations of humpback whales, which carry through water over long distances, vary from one group to another, and change over time. Again, their songs are likely territorial markers and may also have a reproductive function, as in most birds.

Choruses by any species amplify the strength of the group's sound, probably to keep pace with increasing levels of competition from others doing the same. Some individuals use other means of amplification. Woodpeckers and chimpanzees drum on objects in noise-making displays that attract attention and elevate social status. A yellow-bellied sapsucker (woodpecker) male in our clearing taps out not just loud but complex rhythms. He searches for the proper tool to use, twanging on test objects for maximum volume and tenor — tree limbs, stove pipes, the dry boards on the side of my outhouse, or a metal flange wrapped around a hollow apple tree. Having settled on that "instrument," he uses it almost exclusively every day at the start of the breeding season.

Communication enhances power, whether by volume, skill of

performance, accuracy, or originality. But power can be apportioned into different categories. In most birds, it advertises an ability to hold territory that comes from success in finding food, both of which imply suitability for forming a partnership with a potential mate to rear offspring. For wood frog males in a vernal pool, a louder signal increases the range from which females can be attracted. Where breeding spots are highly local and widely distributed (as with frogs who often return to mate and lay eggs in the small fish-free pools where they are born), loudness can be an opportunity for outbreeding. A faint signal by a single male can attract only locals, thus maintaining higher inbreeding and fewer suitable mates.

The increased power derived from teaming up with others can, however, be counterbalanced by increased one-on-one competition. Prairie chickens, grouses, ruffs, and other species famously gather into groups called leks, where females go to compare males in one marketplace, so to speak, so that they can be assured of having choice. Any hopeful male must join the lek to have a possibility of mating, but once there, other selective pressures — particularly females' preferences — come into play for each individual male.

In addition to the advantage of teaming up with others to assert collective power, complementary advantages can include the transfer of information about access to food and safety, as happens in communal bird roosts. In primates, canids, and some insects, communal signals may define and maintain divisions of labor. A communal signal need not be delivered by sound. It just has to activate the sensory system and be unique to the intended group. In the darkness of an insect colony, group identity is maintained by a common scent. A variation in the signal differentiates castes, which perform different tasks.

In fireflies (lampyrid beetles), the males of each species com-
municate their species identity via specific patterns of light
flashes, and receptive females respond with their own patterns of
light flashes. In Southeast Asia, males of some species of fireflies
have now been well documented flashing in synchrony, sometimes
lighting up whole trees. Such behavior is rarer in North America,
but in the Great Smoky Mountains National Park, male fireflies
of one of the nineteen local species, *Photinus carolinus*, also flash
synchronously (at about six flashes per second). The cooperation
of many males perhaps created sufficient stimulus for females,
and also identifies their species among the many others active at
the same time. But I suspect there may be more — females of some
species of carnivorous fireflies respond to signals from males of
other species, not to mate but to capture and eat the males. It
may be strategic for males to approach a female en masse since
she may be a "femme fatale," mimicking a potential mate. But in a
synchronously flashing crowd of males, at least the odds are great
that they are indeed of the right species to mate with.

Among humans, of course, synchronous behavior is commonplace. Examining such behavior in other species helps us to speculate about some of the possible functions of our own behavior.

One evening this past July in the small western Maine town of
Weld, close to 150 people — nearly a third of the town — showed
up at Town Hall as part of the town's bicentennial celebration.
As people mingled, about fifteen fiddlers were jamming by the
stage. Then two couples stepped forward. There was one fiddle
for each pair. One pair also had a piano and an accordion and the
other had a guitar. The bows of the two fiddlers moved in perfect synchrony — not just back and forth but vertically — for long
and fast-moving musical riffs. Their partners kept pace with very

different instruments and with their vocals. The crowd joined the synchrony with hand clapping and foot stomping. Finally, all rose as one to their feet.

At about that same time in July, a little more than eight hundred miles away, a national political convention was taking place. As one of the speakers conducted a mock prosecution of a political rival and invited the audience to render a verdict, the crowd began to respond collectively in a way that probably exceeded in tone what most participants would have been willing to say individually. The group achieved solidarity because of potential competition.

Synchronicity sends a powerful signal. Group identity manifests in a variety of complex ways, some of which directly promote reproduction, others of which may enhance competitive strength against other groups or individuals over territory and resources. In humans, we see it in all sorts of scenarios, from sports to politics to racism and wars . . . to a small community's celebration of its two-hundredth birthday.

What Bees and Flowers Know

New York Times, February 21, 1974

CHARLES DARWIN'S IDEA OF NATURAL SELECTION THROUGH survival of the fittest has been interpreted by some people to mean that life is a free-for-all struggle in which "fitness" is equated with aggression by tooth and claw and the ability to achieve an immediate advantage — as if it were a law of nature, perhaps one that has value and should be obeyed.

However, it concerns neither. It concerns outcomes of what is, from competition as well as cooperation, and among its major outcomes are the adaptations of organisms that have achieved interdependence. This interdependence has evolved not only between individuals but also between species. It has evolved because, like the "games" people play, it has conferred *mutual* benefits on the participants.

In a game both partners attempt to increase their benefit through some symbolic or real gain or profit. In order for both to derive maximum benefit or profit in the long run, it is necessary that the participants adhere to a set of rules. These rules set requirements as well as limits to each other's drives to unlimited increase at the expense of the other. Without imposed or mutually accepted rules, the games played between individuals, between employee and employer, between big business and governments, between different governments, cannot long be played, and both participants lose.

The nature of the players' interactions is often not apparent from casual observation of single "moves," but only from the perspective of time.

Wolves' interaction with the caribou upon which they prey is an example of a long-term game. The wolves' game is to catch caribou, but not the whole herd.

The caribou's game is to evade the wolves. However, if the caribou are too "successful," they may eat up their food supply, destroying their habitat.

The limits within which the wolf-caribou game operates, as with others, have evolved so that neither player has at any one time all of the advantages nor all of the disadvantages. The game, if undisturbed, is obviously a successful one. Wolves have been trotting along the flanks of great herds of caribou in the Arctic for millennia.

In many games, the partner is essentially a renewable resource. The bee and the flower game is another example. The game played by the bee, like that of the wolf, is to gain returns during foraging. If the bees are so successful that they deplete all of the nectar, they will starve, and their population will necessarily stabilize or decline. The flowers' game is to provide food rewards, but not so much that the bees get satiated at one plant, so that they visit and pollinate a large number of flowers. As a result the insects living from the food (sugar and pollen) provided by the flowers are quite often in an "energy crisis."

The interdependence of organisms seldom involves exclusive dominance of one over another. For both to reap maximum benefits in the long run it is required that neither exploit the other fully at any one time. Each absorbs some measure of "cost" in the relationship. The cost can often be deferred, but it can never be eliminated, for doing so destroys the game.

Man at one time was a predator, and his game was similar to that of the wolf with the caribou. However, he did not play by the rules, killing most of the large animals in Eurasia and in America. In part he was able to do this because he used a partner, the domesticated plant (grain). This ally gave him immediate advantages. At first these advantages allowed, and ultimately forced, him to abandon the animal game except on a recreational basis. The rules had been broken, his numbers became too great, and that game ceased to exist.

Our welfare depends in large measure upon domesticated animals and plants, and our game now is more like that of the bee and the flower. Like them, most of the domesticated organisms have long played the game with humans and have become interdependent with us, and the plants cannot reproduce without our aid.

Their strategy, as well as ours, has been good so far. The more of us there are, the more corn and chickens will be raised. These are superbly fit in terms of selection. However, if too many humans are supported by them, and we insist upon continual growth, then the rules of the game will begin to erode. We may find that there is not sufficient space as we use it up to seat some other player.

The game is easily destroyed by help from outside the relationship, for this gives the temporary advantage with which one partner can be, and usually is, eliminated. This is permissible in terms of our own immediate survival — as long as the new partner is reliable. But we are now playing with oil, natural gas, and coal, the nonrenewable chips left by extinct organisms.

If we play this game too intensely it is inevitably programmed to end, perhaps abruptly. Indefinite growth and unlimited exploitation are sooner or later followed by a crash, particularly when the resource is nonrenewable. The greater the growth, the greater the ultimate crash. The optimum state of the game of life necessarily involves cost. We can defer it, but not indefinitely.

Curious Yellow:
A Foray into Iris Behavior

Natural History, May 2015

"PLANT BEHAVIOR" SEEMS LIKE A CONTRADICTION IN TERMS. Animals can react quickly to environmental stimuli, and their reaction by movement qualifies as behavior. Plants generally react so slowly we don't even notice, though there are well-known exceptions, such as the Venus flytrap, which closes to snare insects, and *Mimosa pudica*, whose leaves fold up when jostled by a potential predator. Plants are also rooted in place, which limits their responses. Many, however, have evolved to recruit animals — especially insects, birds, and bats — to assist them, notably for pollination and seed distribution.

As in the mating game of animals, for fertilization to occur in most species of plants, each individual must contrive to get its pollen into the reproductive organ of another of its kind, and in turn to receive such pollen. Animal pollinators need to be rewarded for doing this work, typically with food. The reward must be sufficient but not overly generous. It must be ample enough to lure the pollinator to keep searching for other flowers of the same species, yet it must also be somewhat meager, or the pollinator might use an individual plant as a constant food provider and not move on to transfer pollen to (and from) other plants.

For each individual plant, it is also vital that the pollinator associate the reward with its type of flower — and not rub all the pollen off onto flowers of other species. Prominent identity tags for each plant species, provided by such characteristics as flower color, shape, and scent, ensure that a rewarded pollinator tends to remain flower-faithful. As a consequence, plant species have competed to distinguish themselves from each other, evolving ever-greater differences in their blooms. In short, in handing the *behavior* part of their reproductive life over to animals, plants have generated displays, and some rival those of birds.

One commonplace (but nonetheless gorgeous) example of floral art is the blue flag iris, *Iris versicolor*, widespread in New England wetlands. It has been a favorite of mine ever since, many years ago, I studied its pollination by bumblebees. The long-tongued bee species were the primary pollinators, and their reward was nectar. I shot pretty photographs of their intimate embraces with this flower. Another spectacular iris is *I. atrofusca*, a deep-black one found in the Judaean Desert and nearby arid areas. My Israeli friend and fellow evolutionary ecologist Avishai Shmida introduced it to me. The species is pollinated by solitary bees that use the flowers as an overnighting den. The early morning sun heats the flowers, and so the bees sheltered inside them get warmed up and have a jump-start on their day of visiting other flowers. Reward enough! Meanwhile the plant possibly gains in water balance by not producing nectar. My northern bumblebees, in contrast, need sugar as a fuel to shiver and keep warm.

The yellow, or yellow flag, iris (*I. pseudacorus*), native in Europe, western Asia, and northwest Africa, is, like the North American blue flag iris, at home in wetlands. To my great surprise and pleasure I found a single plant of it in bloom directly along the Atlantic shoreline, on Star Island, at the border between New Hampshire and Maine. I could not resist taking a piece of its root and transplanting it. A lush plant of it now grows at my camp in Maine, and there in the summer of 2014 it flowered splendidly under my "shower" (a garden watering can that hangs from a sugar maple tree), a place where I spent days watching the nesting behavior of tree swallows in an adjacent bird box.

Day after day, and then week after week, watching swallows fly in and out of their box, I could not fail to notice the yellow iris plant beside my perch. It always had one or more large flower buds, only one or more flowers that were open, and increasing

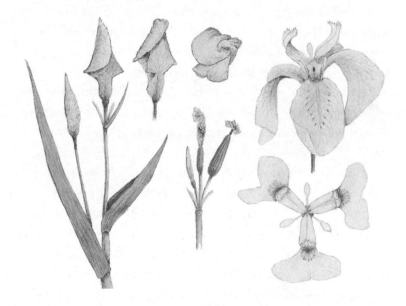

Sketches of yellow iris buds (at left), and stages leading to "instant" flower opening.

numbers of curled-up spent flowers and seed capsules. Curiously, though, there never seemed to be a bud transitioning into a flower!

Something didn't add up — until one day when I glanced down and noticed a flower bud, and then, literally in the next moment, looked again and saw a fully open flower in its place. It couldn't be magic. To find out what had happened, I then started to monitor the flowers more closely, to be there when other buds opened and to make dissections to construct a working model of how a bud could move its parts to transform itself into full flower in a flash.

In all *Iris* species, the characteristic bloom is divided into thirds. Each third has a large drooping petal known as a "fall"; a vertical and often nearly equally showy petal called a "standard"; a stamen (comprising the male structures); and a pistil (the female structures). The fall has a greatly enlarged hanging lip and markings that serve as a "nectar guide," which helps orient pollinators on their way into a tubular chamber where they access the nectar. The roof of this tube is formed by the style, or shaft, of the pistil. In most flowers the style is a simple rod, but in irises it is flattened and flanged at the sides. The shaft bears the stigma, which receives pollen as a pollinator enters. As the pollinator passes, it also picks up pollen from the anther, located under the style.

An iris bud, in contrast to the flower, is spikelike, with all the parts of the triple array tightly rolled together and wrapped inside.

I noticed that the stem holding a flower bud extended in length as the bud developed, so that the bud reached above the two leaf bracts that had surrounded it the day before. Subsequently, several hours before opening, the flower bud expanded near the base. A top view showed the three outer petals — the falls — curled into a swirl, wound around each other near their tips. When it happened, the opening of the bud took about one second, the three falls flying to the sides and down to nearly full extension, leaving the three "standards" upright.

The bloom remained fresh for two days, after which the three petals again coalesced into a coil around each other and then shrank. The ovary grew and the remains of the petals dried and fell off. The blue flag iris followed the same general pattern but lacked the "instant" quickness of flower-opening behavior.

The mechanism of flower opening and closing and other movement in plants, such as *Mimosa* leaf movements, involves volume changes in different compartments that expand or shrink as water is shifted in or out by osmosis, which depends in part on uptake of sugars after conversion from polysaccharide. However, both growth and osmotic pressure changes are gradual processes and do not explain the mechanics of *sudden* movements in *I. pseudacorus*. The snap of petal extension would require prior storage of energy, followed by a trigger mechanism for its release, perhaps similar to the way a number of plant species forcibly eject seeds: the common jewelweed (*Impatiens capensis*), for example, can throw seeds several yards from its fruit capsule.

Sudden movements resulting from release of stored energy are common in arthropods, including mantid shrimp (order Stomatopoda), jumping spiders, and jumping insects such as fleas, flea beetles, leafhoppers, and springtails (as well as the back-flipping click beetle). Slow muscle contraction stores energy in a mechanical spring, and then releases it by a trigger mechanism analogous to that of a crossbow. A holding mechanism is required to store the energy. In the case of the yellow iris, the folded bud is apparently held in place by the fall petals, wrapped around each other near their tips. The stable position persists until sufficient force builds up to release the falls; as they start to slip over each other they open all the way. How might the instant-opening behavior be accomplished, and is it a possible adaptation for pollination? Since the iris flower evolved under the selective pressure of pollinators, and its main pollinators are bumblebees, it is necessary to see how the flower is constructed to attract as well as use them.

Each flower's fall petal has two nectaries at its base, each yielding up to two microliters (that is, two millionths of a liter) of nectar, which is not enough to satiate a big bee but probably enough to stimulate her to search for another flower of the same kind. But not every bee reacts alike. A naive bee beginning her foraging career samples almost any kind of flower she comes in contact with. In order to become "converted" to a particular kind of flower (as well as to its plant's associated habit), it is important that the *first* ones she encounters have a high food reward. Subsequently, after she is converted to it, as from another flower kind, she can continue in part on expectation. On the other hand, if she frequently encounters empty flowers of that type and in those locations, after a while she will learn to avoid them and visit others instead.

Perhaps the ancestors of the yellow iris became widely distributed in a very patchy way, say, in scattered wetlands, where cross-pollination was difficult. Under that circumstance, it was crucial that bees attracted to the flower not be disappointed. One way to improve the odds was to make sure the flower didn't flash its signal until the reward was definitely in place, so that she would not right off encounter empty, unrewarding flowers.

When I told this to a friend she immediately responded, "It's like a yard or estate sale — where you put up a huge sign to raise high expectations. But you can't put up the sign until *all* of the goods are out." As she pointed out, the most motivated customers try to get there first, streaming in before others. But if there's little on display, and they don't find something they want, they leave — and you lose them.

It's the same with an iris. Although the flower bud is itself potentially a big colorful sign, a bee isn't likely to confuse it with the real sign, the open flower with its nectar guide. But if the flower petals open slowly, then it's like putting up the sign before the goods are available. Naive bee customers will be attracted from afar, look, see no nectar guide, no sign where the "door" is, and leave, never to heed that sign again.

As in other iris species, stranded individual yellow irises would still have reproduced (or grown) by means of rhizomes — horizontal underground stems — creating patches of what really were clones. A clone patch would make cross-pollination even more difficult, because bees tend to stay in a good flower patch when they find one. Nevertheless, the yellow iris would keep open its option for sexual reproduction.* Producing seeds by self-pollination can afford the plant some advantage. But in the long run, "selfing" is an evolutionary dead end because in nature, change is constant.

---

* Subsequently, by performing surgical operations on unopened flower buds, I confirmed the here-suggested mechanism of the iris flower's opening. But the adaptive significance remains speculative.

Twists and Turns

Natural History, November 2015

I HAVE STUDIED IRIS FLOWERS BECAUSE I GOT HOOKED BY
an incidental observation: the bud of an iris changing, in a fraction of a second, into a large, complex, showy flower. The grip of
the petals, necessary to store the energy for the petals' eventual
flip outward as the bud opens, depends on their twist around each
other. At first I thought that the direction of the twist seemed irrelevant. From a couple of sketches that I had made, however, I
noticed the petals unfurled in a counterclockwise direction. That
seemed odd. Now the direction of the twist had my attention. I
made counts in the flower patch next to my cabin, expecting to see
roughly equal numbers of clockwise and counterclockwise twists,
since the direction would make no difference in the workability of
the mechanism. However, for each of the twenty-six flower buds I
examined, the petal twists were oriented the same way: counterclockwise! How do flowers "know" how to always turn left? Why?

Iris pseudacoris has a suite of features that are uniformly in-
variant — for example, three banner and three flag petals that are

universally yellow — but those are expected adaptations. What possible value or difference could bud-handedness be — for pollination, for bumblebees, or for anything else — when that feature is obliterated the moment the flower opens? The uniformity of the twist could not be a matter of random chance, nor did it seem an adaptation.

Biology is in large part history, which is what separates it from physics and chemistry. And to gain a historical perspective into any specific biological pattern requires seeing where else the phenomenon may be found, and then asking if the pattern is associated with any of a large number of environmental factors that may have been in common or different with respect to a related species. The blood iris, *Iris sanguina*, native to Asia, and now in our yard, was next to a large number of the native blue flag, *I. versicolor*. I examined both, sampling twenty-three and fifteen flower buds, respectively. The results were identical for both species: the twist of the flower buds was 100 percent counterclockwise, suggesting that this odd trait was perhaps traceable to iris ancestors. Comparison with still other plant species was necessary to see if the trait could be traced to more distant forebears.

Both scarlet runner beans (*Phaseolus coccineus*) on poles along our garden fence and common morning glories (*Ipomoea purpurea*) in our field have climbing vines. A vine has four options: spiral either clockwise or counterclockwise in response to some feature of the substrate, go straight up, or twist willy-nilly. Only the twist as such has an adaptive function, and as expected, the sixteen runner beans I examined wound their way up everything they encountered — fence, grass stems, bushes, goldenrod, each other — but all twirling counterclockwise. The signal for the winding was contact; when the growing vine tips were unobstructed they went straight. Of the seventy morning glories sampled, all, without exception, also twisted counterclockwise. And fifty night-shade vines (*Solanum dulcamara*) at another site by the garden proved to be uniformly twirled counterclockwise as well.

Unanimity in twist direction — supposedly a neutral trait — in 236 individuals of four different plant families, Iridaceae, Faba-ceae, Convolvulaceae, and Solanaceae, seemed odd, unless they shared a still more ancient common ancestor. But why did that ancestor have *that* characteristic, and the descendants retain it? In all these plant families, the twist at least had a function, even though the direction — the point of interest — didn't matter. The functions happened to be flower bud opening in the first species, and support for climbing to the light in the other three.

Trees, however, provide their own support. They should have no reason to do the twist — but I decided to check.

I noticed cracks in the dry logs of my cabin walls and ceil-ings. The cracks ran along the length of the logs, sometimes with a slant. I made a count: forty-eight logs showed no cracks run-ning in a slant direction; twenty-seven did, and they ran counter-clockwise, and only one was clockwise. Trees hoist their leaves on branches to the sunlight with their own trunks. Yet they were still twisting in the same direction, as though it was part of their basic makeup.

Why might something as seemingly irrelevant as twist direction have become ingrained? When I Googled "directional movement in plants," I learned that counterclockwise movement by climbing vines was thought to be unique to the Northern Hemisphere be-cause of the "Coriolis effect." If so, then there should be a clockwise twist in the Southern Hemisphere.

However, the idea of the Coriolis effect turns out to be myth in-vented apparently as a rationalization. In 2007, Will Edwards of James Cook University in Cairns, Australia, along with fellow researchers, determined that, globally, the direction of plant twists was affected neither by locality nor latitude. Well, mine were certainly all growing at the same latitude, and had the same twist. Then I encountered the work of Maria Stolarz, of Sklodowska University in Lublin, Poland, who published research on the physiological, cellular, and molecular basis of the twirling motion of plants, as influenced by light, temperature, and other factors. However, she did not mention the direction of twisting. Yes, the environment's effect is strong. As I mentioned, in the vines that I had examined, the twirling occurred only in response to contact with vertical objects; otherwise, the growth trajectories were straight.

We can suppose the earliest plants had a specific twist simply by the randomness of the draw due to a common origin. However, if it made no difference to their fitness, the logical conclusion from an evolutionary perspective is that anything not needed, such as the specific direction of the twist, would eventually become abolished. It would be retained in the long run only if it were beneficial. The evidence is ample: the counterclockwise twist was not abolished. It is widely and prominently exhibited. Therefore, it cannot exist now due to random chance. Yet there seemed to be no obvious selective advantage to right versus left as such. Something else besides natural selection on the plants seemed to operate to maintain the twist! We must look, I thought, to the historical and chemical underpinnings themselves, in the structure of life.

The genetic code is read off one strand of the DNA molecule in one direction as the double helix unwinds to be copied via messenger RNA. It seems curious, though, that the DNA molecule is not exactly analogous to a zipper. Instead, it is a spiral. Furthermore, the DNA double helix reputedly twists counterclockwise (but is often claimed to be drawn incorrectly), as does RNA (which is normally single-stranded) when it is crystallized. And the fact that all twenty amino acids in our and in plant proteins are only of left-handed orientation is suspect. Why *left*-handed? All of this is taken as evidence of the idea that all of life on earth branched from *one* common ancestor. This makes sense.

However, as far as I know, there is no known connection between a plant's twist direction and amino acid orientation. Might there be one?

The handedness of humans, as well as the counterclockwise twist of a vine, are under at least genetic influence, if not control. However, no controlling genes of twist direction have been identified. By default, we therefore interpret the twist as being controlled by many genes. What if, instead of many genes, it is not genes at all but the nature of the molecules of living things biased toward a *consensus* of mirror images of certain molecules that is required to smoothly operate biochemical machinery and which then have repercussions on overall bio-tissue construction, function, and reproduction? Just as bricks of uniform, rather than random, lengths facilitate building construction, and just as snail shells all twirl in the same direction because the odd ones can't mate, perhaps our molecular building blocks are matched to a certain directionality of the organism for optimal growth and function.

This view does not mean that chance and history had no role to play in the evolution of the twist. Perhaps a mere twist — any twist — in the chain of molecules was favored for a biomechanics advantage in the first molecules of life. It may have provided momentum of the reactions and an increase in efficiency — especially if there was a consistent twist in a specific direction that in turn translated to a bias in the orientation of the amino acids being accepted into the growing amino acid chain. Experiments might tell, but the DNA we have now is all we have to go on. We don't have any with an opposite DNA twist to test on oppositely twisted remaining molecules required to build the organism.

Whenever we "make" DNA, we copy it off *existing* strands — we replicate a 3.4-billion-year-old script. As far as I know, we cannot yet make artificial DNA and RNA molecules twist in the opposite direction, and then present them with a choice of right- and left-handed amino acids, to see if the protein made would then preferentially incorporate amino acids of one direction or the other. If we could then feed this new protein to an iris plant or a vine, we might watch with rapt attention to see if the twist then changes to the opposite direction.

We are composed of billions of these molecules and they all face one direction. The twist of the two strands that make up the DNA molecule happens to be counterclockwise. Perhaps on some other planet it is clockwise.

The commonness of the counterclockwise twist in the ultimate product, the plant body itself, started me down a long rambling road with many twists and turns — from the microscopic to the cosmic — until I acquired one more data point. Or perhaps it was fifty-six points. Ironically, it was a weed in our garden that eased my mind considerably (although by no means completely). I thank my lucky stars for this weed, and for my penchant to try to get a second opinion or, better yet, another fact.

Black bindweed, *Polygonum convolvulus*, is a creeping-climbing weed with leaves and vines and associated habits of growth that seem nearly identical to those of the morning glory. They are currently placed in two different plant families, Polygonaceae and Convolvulaceae. Bindweed flowers are tiny and white, and the plant is not in the least eye-catching. But as I saw one draped over a blueberry bush and began pulling it off, I suddenly realized its potential.

Like the morning glory, the bindweed sends runners in straight lines in all directions, and here and there, where it contacts a bush or a grass stalk, it sends a tendril curling its way up to display its flowers. My *Polygonum* specimen appeared to twirl exactly like the morning glory. I photographed the two side by side to show the identical plant strategy. But when I unwound the bindweed vine from the goldenrod stalk it had climbed, I needed to turn it counterclockwise. It had been wound *clockwise!* I looked again, again, again. And then I pulled up every one I could find, fifty-six to be exact. Every single one was wound up clockwise. To be absolutely sure I had not been wrong before, I revisited the morning glories, and the beans, and brought a couple dozen of them in to spread on my desk, to compare them side by side. There was no doubting the difference in the directions of the twirls.

I was grateful indeed that this little weed saved me from possibly grand delusions. Nevertheless, the wonder of the 236 individuals of four plant families agreeing on such a trivial point as the direction of the twist is compelling, even though how they ended up that way remains unanswered.

CODA

Writing this piece revealed to me assumptions that must be clarified to avoid confusion. There is no confusion about the essential point of chirality, namely, that an asymmetrical object can be twisted in either of two forms that, like our right and left hands, cannot fit as identical copies one on top of the other. We are not confused between our right versus our left hand, nor between clockwise versus counterclockwise turns on a clock, simply because of assumptions of what we are looking at, and from where. We all assume we are looking at our hands with our own body as reference, and we are looking at the face of a clock and the direction of the moving hand of it, starting from the 12 going to our right and not the 6 going to our left. But from where is the twist of the DNA molecule, an amino acid molecule, or a vine, or a galaxy in space, viewed?

The descriptive terms "right-handed" versus "left-handed" and "clockwise" versus "counterclockwise" are routinely applied as from some imagined location of the viewer. We are naturally used to thinking of clockwise as the direction of the hands of a clock moving to the right as we look down at the clock face. But in the twist of a vine around a pole, the direction is not only lateral but also vertical. If we watch the vine from the perspective of it climbing up the pole, it is turning one way, but if we instead follow the same twist going *down* toward the roots, it is then turning counter to that direction, or counterclockwise.

The spiral DNA molecules of living things indeed all twist in the same direction, specified as clockwise or right-handed, but as DNA is made, it grows in one direction, and when the strands unwind (as in the synthesis of RNA), they twist in the opposite. Which is "clockwise"? In the winding up or unwinding direction? Similarly, amino acids, the building blocks of protein, exist analogously to our hands, with a "thumb" (a particular formation called a carboxyl group) angled to one side or the other with respect to the rest of the molecule. They are differentiated as L versus D amino acids, representing L for levo (left-handed) and D for dextro (right-handed). The distinction between them, however, is not fundamentally different from the way we designate the twist of a screw: whether we call that twist right-handed (D) or left-handed (L) depends on how we see the twist — whether we follow it toward or away from us. Screws are, I believe, *considered* clockwise-turning. By convention, all the screws we now make are tightened in the same way. Similarly, because the life that exists now on earth developed from the same origin, the chirality of DNA, amino acid molecules, and vine-turning are also history-based; therefore a correlation from the molecular to the organismal could be expected, but whether we call it right or left is not a matter of right or wrong.

Birds Coloring Their Eggs

Previously published as "Why Is a Robin's Egg Blue?"
Audubon, July 1986

THE FOUR EGGS OF THE SCARLET TANAGER, IN A CUP OF loose twigs lined with rootlets, are sky blue and spotted with light brown in a ring at the larger end. The four eggs of the eastern pec wee are a light cream, with a wreath of dark reddish-brown and lavender spots about the larger end. These colors are set against a perfectly round nest cup decorated with gray-green lichens. Woodpecker and kingfisher eggs, from holes excavated in trees and sandbanks, respectively, are translucent white without any markings. Why would others be in endlessly varying colors, inscribed with dots, blotches, squiggles, and dabs of indelible black, amber, army green, brick red, apricot, purple, brown paint on white, aqua, blue, or beige? The different colors, or lack of them, are products of evolution. What were the selective pressures that produced them?

The combinations of markings and colors on birds' eggs seem like creativity gone berserk. Why should the color of an eggshell matter to a bird? Why, indeed, have any color at all? There must have been reasons to add the color, or else specialized glands to apply it would not have evolved. So why are robins' eggs blue, flickers' eggs white, and loons' eggs dark olive green?

Birds' eggs are marked by pigments secreted from the walls of the oviduct. The egg remains uncolored until just before being laid; when it traverses the uterus, where the pressure of the egg squeezes the pigment from uterine glands onto the eggshell, and the motion of the egg produces the color patterns. It is as if innumerable brushes hold still while the canvas moves. If the egg remains still, there are spots, and if it moves while the glands continue secreting, then lines and scrawls result.

Egg color is under genetic control, and there is considerable genetic plasticity. Strains of domestic chickens have been developed that lay eggs tinted blue, green, and olive, as well as the more familiar white and brown.

It is not surprising that Charles Darwin, with his wide-ranging interests, also thought about the adaptive significance of the coloration of birds' eggs. Since coloration is generally absent in hole-nesters such as woodpeckers, parrots, kingfishers, barbets, and honey guides, he supposed that the pigmentation on the eggs of open-nesters acts as a sunscreen to protect the embryo. But that does not explain the diversity of bird egg artistry. The British ornithologist David Lack, in turn, believed the white coloration of eggs of hole-nesters allowed the birds to see their eggs in the dark. However, even if it is advantageous for birds to see their eggs in the dark (which I doubt), we are *still* left to explain the tremendous differences in colors and patterns found, especially in the species that do not nest in holes. Why isn't one sunscreen best? And if so, why don't all use it? And why are some hole-nesters' eggs spotted?

. . .

Experiments confirm that the color of some birds' eggs conceals them from predators. In a famous experiment, the renowned Dutch ethnologist Niko Tinbergen distributed equal numbers of the naturally khaki-colored spotted eggs of black-headed gulls and white eggs near a gull colony and then recorded the predation by carrion crows and herring gulls on these unguarded eggs. The naturally colored eggs suffered the least predation.

We might reasonably assume that the color of snipe, killdeer, and gull eggs is adaptive for camouflage, and that it evolved under selective pressure from visually oriented egg predators. But why, then, do other ground-nesting birds — most ducks and many grouse — have pale unmarked eggs that cannot be considered camouflaged by any stretch of the imagination? Perhaps part of the answer is that most of these birds hide their nests in dense vegetation. Also, the incubating female's own body is a camouflage blanket. Perhaps these exceptions prove a rule.

So far, so good. But there is a hitch. Ducks and grouselike birds usually lay more than a dozen eggs per clutch. If the female started to sit on the eggs as soon as the first ones were laid, in order to hide them, the chicks would hatch out over a period of up to two weeks. It is necessary for the eggs to hatch synchronously, and to accomplish this, the hen must stay off the eggs until the last one is laid. So how are the eggs protected from predators? A pet mallard hen gave me a hint. She built a nest by scraping leaves to gather under a bush by the front window. Being well fed, she laid enormous clutches of creamy pale-green eggs. But I never saw the eggs directly. Each morning before she left, after laying an egg, she used her bill to pull leaves from around the nest to cover the eggs completely. The leaves were better camouflage than spots on the eggs or her own body could ever be. I do not know if all ducks and grouse cover their eggs in a similar manner but their nests are usually mere depressions, with loose vegetation that could serve as a cover. Not all ground-nesting birds have uncamouflaged eggs, though. Those of the willow and rock ptarmigans, for example, are heavily blotched and marbled with blackish-brown.

Many birds with nests that have no loose material with which to cover the eggs also have, like hole-nesters, pure white eggs. They include hummingbirds, pigeons, and doves. But these birds lay only two eggs per clutch, and they start to incubate as soon as the first egg is laid, so none of their eggs are normally left uncovered.

The best explanation for the lack of color and markings on hole-nesters' eggs and those of birds that lay small clutches is probably simply that there was no need for color, so none evolved. Yet, as already mentioned, there are birds that nest in holes that do lay spotted eggs. All of *these* birds, however, build nests inside the holes. (True hole-nesters such as woodpeckers excavate their own holes and lay white eggs without adding any nest material.) I suspect, therefore, that these spots are evolutionary baggage. They tell us that these birds had previously been open-nesters who switched to hole-nesting, and they retained the habit of building nests (as well as the coloration of their eggs) because there was no great selective pressure for change.

While coloring and markings serve as camouflage, the diversity of egg coloring requires further explanation. Some bird egg markings function to make them stand out like a red flag. On our Atlantic and Pacific coasts and in Europe, there are murres that nest on the ledges and sea cliffs in colonies of hundreds of thousands. Several species of colonial cliff-nesting murres (as well as the extinct great auk) have eggs that, between individuals, vary endlessly in colors and markings. The ground color of the eggs varies from creamy to white, reddish, warm ocher, pale bluish, or even deep greenish-blue. The markings upon this ground color, in turn, may be blotches, spots, or intricate interlacing lines of yellowish-brown, bright red, dark brown, or black. The eggs of some individuals are unmarked. (When a murre loses the one egg — its entire clutch — it lays another, and this one is colored like the first.) In contrast, the eggs of the closely related auklets of various species, which nest in burrows or rock crevices, have few or no markings. As an analogy for the individuality of murre egg coloring, I consider the markings of lobster pots along the coast of Maine, where the harbors and inlets are dotted with the floats of thousands of lobster traps. There are green floats, red floats, white floats, striped red-white floats, and so on. The large numbers of traps and the featureless environment of the open water make it impractical for a lobsterer to find his or her own traps by remembering their precise locations. Each lobsterer therefore uses a different color pattern for floats in order to quickly home in on and identify their own.

Chester A. Reed, one of the early "oologists" during the heyday of egg collecting in the early twentieth century, says of the murres: "The eggs are laid as closely as possible on the ledges where the incubating birds sit upright, in long rows like an army on guard. As long as each bird succeeds in finding an egg to cover on its return home, it is doubtful if the bird either knows, or cares, whether it is its own or not." Thanks to experiments some twenty-five years ago by Beat Tschantz of the Zoological Institute of the University of Bern, Switzerland, we know that Reed was wrong. The murres no more incubate one another's eggs than the Maine lobsterers tend one another's traps. Both use color and markings to identify their property, as Tschantz showed by switching eggs in nests and finding that if an egg of a different color or marking pattern was substituted for the bird's own egg, that egg was rejected, but another egg with a similar pattern was accepted. Nevertheless, birds don't have innate recognition on their own eggs. For example, if a murre's egg is marked with white feces in small increments, the bird learns the new color pattern and will reject eggs of its own original pattern. The egg discrimination by murres stands in strong contrast to the behavior of some birds — herring gulls, for example — which accept almost anything of any color even remotely resembling an egg, presumably because their uniquely placed nests are adequate orientation for returning without fail to their own eggs. Recognition of eggs by their color pattern has evolved in some other birds under an entirely different set of selective pressures: the need to detect and destroy the eggs of parasite birds.

Reproductive success in murres is enhanced if the females can pick out their own uniquely colored eggs. In contrast, under the selective pressure of brood parasitism, a bird's reproductive success is enhanced if it can recognize the eggs of *other* birds, those in its own clutch, to be able to discriminate against them and discard them. The possibility of parasitism creates selective pressure on the host bird to detect the odd-colored eggs, which in turn leads to an evolving arms race because it puts pressure on the parasite to evolve eggs marked to resemble those of its host.

The European cuckoo and its hosts may have evolved the most sophisticated matching of egg color. It never builds a nest of its own. Among the various birds it victimizes are wagtails, which have white eggs densely spotted in gray; bramblings, whose pale-blue eggs have heavy reddish spots; and European redstarts, with blue unspotted eggs. The cuckoo eggs found in these nests usually closely match those of their hosts. The accuracy of the imitations is sometimes so good that even the human eye has difficulty in distinguishing the eggs of the parasite from those of the host.

It was long a mystery how such color matching could occur, for surely cuckoos do not paint their eggs to match those of their intended victims. The real answer, however, is almost as bizarre: in any given area, the cuckoos are made up of reproductively isolated subgroups called gentes, whose females restrict their parasitism to particular hosts. It is believed that the gentes arose through geographic isolation, although at the present time two or more gentes may occupy the same area. A given female always lays the same-colored eggs, and almost always places them with the same host species. The mechanism by which this is made possible is still not well understood. However, the behaviors of laying eggs into the nests of specific birds, and the physiology of laying the specifically matching eggs to that species, are inherited. They have become sex-linked on a *female* chromosome. In essence, the cuckoo population has seven different "kinds" of females who look alike, but behave and color their eggs differently. It goes without saying that in all of the parasitized species, the females are scrupulous in rejecting cuckoo eggs that do not closely match their own. The selective pressure for such behavior has been great, because cuckoos are large in size relative to their hosts and as such their young need to usurp all of the allo-parents' foraging effort to be reared to adulthood. As a consequence, these young cuckoos always roll the others eggs out of the nest they find themselves in.

In European passerine birds heavily parasitized by cuckoos, there has been potent selective pressure to foil the parasitism. Hosts have developed a strong attention to egg color code, abandoning many nests with cuckoo eggs or throwing the cuckoo eggs out. This puts stronger pressure on the cuckoos to produce even better egg mimicry.

Parasitism in North America is no less severe, but the principal parasite of songbirds, the brown-headed cowbird, thus far has not evolved egg color mimicry. Nevertheless, the cowbird is a highly successful parasite. It is one of the most common of our native passerine birds, and it is also one of the most widely distributed. According to Herbert Friedmann, a longtime student of avian brood parasitism, it parasitizes more than 350 species and subspecies of birds. Some species suffer heavily. Up to 78 percent of all song sparrow nests in some areas have been victimized by this parasite. The cowbird, however, also lays eggs occasionally in the nests of such unlikely potential hosts as the spotted sandpiper and ruby-crowned kinglet, as well as in many other nests where its eggs regularly get damaged or evicted. In short, it wastes many eggs. The cowbird is partial to open habitat, having spread east from the short-grass prairies in the Midwest only over the past two or three centuries.

California quail and spotted towhee laid eggs into the same nest (drawn from a photograph).

At this point in the egg evolutionary arms race, only some of the potential victims of the brown-headed cowbird have evolved appropriate egg-rejection responses. Stephen I. Rothstein of the University of California at Santa Barbara determined this by making plaster of Paris eggs and painting them to mimic cowbird eggs. He deposited these in a total of 640 nests of forty-three species and found that two-thirds of the passerine birds accepted the parasite eggs, while only one-fourth consistently rejected them. Some birds, like the red-winged blackbird, yellow warbler, phoebe, and barn swallow, consistently accepted both fake and real parasite eggs, while others, like the catbird, robin, and kingbird, consistently rejected them. Since the birds were consistent "acceptors" or "rejectors," Rothstein speculated that once the rejection behavior was genetically coded, it was of such great advantage that it spread rapidly and became fixed.

Given that cowbirds as a species parasitize nests of birds with little discrimination, it could be hit or miss whether in any parasitization they waste their reproductive effort and resources, or enhance them. However, cowbirds may pay attention to the nestlings' survival by checking back to see if the nests they have parasitized are successful. This permits them to learn to differentiate those where their eggs fail versus those where they succeed. Given continual coevolution, it can be expected that the nest parasite would narrow its choices to specific species with which it experiences the best reproductive payoff. In turn, that species will experience strong selective pressure to discriminate against accepting eggs, resulting in ever-closer egg mimicry. For the cowbird it is camouflage of its eggs not only against the environment of leaves and pebbles of earth, but against other eggs too.

Early on in the relationship between parasite and potential host, a lack of color matching of the eggs is probably not necessary to ensure the parasite's success. However, eventually, as with the European cuckoo, similarity becomes important. It is doubtful if rejection can occur if — initially by chance and ultimately by evolution — the parasite and host eggs are exactly alike. Indeed, song sparrows and brown-headed cowbirds have eggs that are similar in size and dense brown spotting; and this sparrow rarely rejects the cowbird eggs. Both robins and catbirds, which have immaculate blue eggs, on the other hand, almost always do. In contrast, phoebes, which lay pure white eggs, readily accept cowbird eggs. But does a phoebe, nesting under a ledge or on a beam under a barn, ever notice the color of its eggs at all?

Since a key component of defense against parasitism involves egg recognition, one would predict that means of detecting foreign eggs would evolve. For example, it would be easier to recognize a stranger's egg if all the eggs within a clutch were similar. Does this help explain the fact that songbirds subject to parasitism have uniform egg coloring between eggs within the *same* clutch, whereas hawks, eagles, and ravens, who are seldom if ever subject to nest parasitism, can afford to have a variety of egg colorations within one clutch?

Bernhard Rensch, studying mimicry of cuckoo eggs in Germany, wondered whether songbirds could recognize their own eggs. In one experiment he replaced the first three eggs in a nest of the garden warbler with lesser whitethroat eggs. The warbler then ejected its own fourth egg! Rensch concluded that egg rejection was not on the basis of true recognition of a bird's own eggs, but on the basis of the discordance in appearance relative to the other eggs in the nest. Similar experiments by Rothstein now show that songbirds also learn the appearance of their own eggs, becoming imprinted on the first egg they see in their nest. In an experiment that showed this most clearly, Rothstein removed all eggs in a catbird nest each day as they were laid, replacing them with cowbird eggs. Although catbirds normally reject cowbird eggs placed in with their own, his catbird accepted a whole clutch of cowbird eggs. Then a single catbird egg added to the cowbird eggs was rejected.

Likely one of the most widespread parasitizations occurs when females deposit eggs in other nests *within the same species,* where the eggs would automatically blend in. The eggs would match "perfectly," and good and compatible care would be *ensured* — as if families who had kids who looked like identical twins to others' kids could pawn them off on anybody who already had some of the same age.

Rearing of offspring from others of the same species probably happens often in birds, though we would normally not detect it. I think a particular species of the colonial weaverbirds of Africa offers one of the best examples. In contrast to most others that nest solitarily, various females within the same colony of village weavers (*Ploceus capitatus*) lay eggs of *different* colors. As though they were different species, one individual may lay green eggs, another blue, another rust-colored, and another uncolored. As with the cuckoos, each female always lays the same distinctively colored eggs throughout its life. The nests are close together, making it potentially easy for a female to monitor a neighboring nest and lay an egg into it at the right time. Thus the tendency to do so, by mistake or otherwise, would be adaptive, since it would result in more eggs of that individual being nurtured, provided that egg dumping is not detected and the odd egg removed.

To envision how the large variety of egg coloring evolved in this colonial weaverbird, suppose that a mutation produced a female who laid green eggs where the others all laid white eggs. Before the mutation, the female carrying it might not have been able to identify a parasite egg in her nest. But laying odd-colored eggs relative to her neighbors, she may be the only one in the colony who can *avoid* being parasitized (although she cannot also practice parasitism). These birds indeed use egg color as a cue to eject conspecific foreign eggs.

It will likely not be possible ever to say with any degree of precision why a robin's egg is blue or a kingbird's egg is white and splotched with dark brown and purple. However, the diversity of patterns indicates a variety of selective pressures at work. The coloration of birds' eggs reflects organization in many evolutionary paths that we now see in different stages. This, in turn, colors the mind as well as the eye, and gives eggs an additional beauty that no person's brush could ever impart.

Birds, Bees, and Beauty: Adaptive Aesthetics

Natural History, March 2017

BEAUTY INVOLVES SO MANY PIVOTAL AND INSTINCTIVE AS-pects of life that we might accept it, as is, without defining it or considering its evolution. The topic is old and starts simply enough with iconic examples such as the huge tail on a peacock, the brilliant plumage on birds of paradise, and the elegant structures built by bowerbirds.

In *The Descent of Man, and Selection in Relation to Sex*, published in 1871, Darwin posited that these extravagant male displays resulted through selection by female choice. Seventy-eight years earlier, in 1793, Christian Konrad Sprengel concluded in his book *Das entdeckte Geheimnis der Natur in Bau und der Befruchtung der Blumen* (*The Discovered Secret of Nature in the Construction and Fertilization of Flowers*) that the colors, scents, and shapes of flowers are meant not for our eyes but for bees that are attracted to them and serve to fertilize them. Sprengel's astonishing discovery languished in obscurity mainly because his contemporary, the eminent writer-philosopher-poet Johann Wolfgang von Goethe, roundly ridiculed this idea of pollination (bees working for the benefit of flowers, and flowers rewarding them with nectar) as an intrusion of proximate, silly human rationality.

Sprengel's idea would not make sense to human rationality until the mechanics of evolution by adaptation had been worked out, or at least enunciated, and distinctions could be made between proximate and ultimate causation. However, even Darwin, in his original thesis of "survival of the fittest," could apparently find no reason why the peacock's long ponderous tail could make the animal more fit. The opposite — that it saddled the bearer with a huge cost — seemed true instead.

It made no sense to assign fitness benefits to what is potentially a serious cost, especially if it were selected by *arbitrary* choice, which by that logic could just as well have been *un*costly, or better still, even adaptive. Should not females evolve to prefer males with small, light tails — which promote adroit and efficient flight to better escape predators — so that their offspring would inherit the same benefit, instead of a burden? Female choice based on aesthetic attraction to features that were handicaps didn't make proximal sense. To solve the problem, which seemed to challenge his central idea of survival of the fittest, Darwin put aesthetic attraction into a different bin. He invented a separate category that he labeled "sexual selection." In doing so, he singled it out as something separate from what he, and Alfred Russel Wallace, thought of as "natural selection." Nevertheless, sexual selection is no less natural than habitat selection, food selection, home selection, or selection of anything else that promotes survival and reproduction. All are based on preference and choice. All selection is natural, whether related to fleeing, fighting, mating, nesting, migrating, or feeding.

The results of natural selection based on aesthetics may often appear to be neutral or even anti-fitness, but that may be simply because it is *interpreted proximally*, without taking ultimate benefits into account. Consider again the peacock's monstrous tail and the woodcock's exuberant sky dance in spring. They are undoubtedly energy-costly and predator-attracting. However, investment in these traits is the price these males must pay to propel their genes into the next generation. Females who select mates with these traits will have offspring that also have these mate preferences and traits. Although such selection increases the death rate of some participants and decreases the reproduction of most, it correspondingly greatly increases the number of young sired by the few that have the trait. Fitness always refers simply to those that succeed, not to those that fail in the genetic lottery, and in this case the pertinent environment where that selection is played out is that of males facing mate-selection competition from others. Therefore, the trait that may kill many males is a fitness marker that females choose to maximize passing on their genes (and that males must acquire for *their* genetic fitness). And to do that they are led by their aesthetic choices, no less than birds' choices of which colored eggs they reject from their clutches, or which habitats they choose or which color of berries they eat.

The issue is not whether an aesthetic signal leads to fitness for the *species;* it is whether or not it signals fitness for the *individuals* of it. However, a more profound question is how a population of many individuals agrees to or converges upon *one* very specific and seemingly arbitrary model that appeals to all. That this process happens routinely seems at first glance remarkable. Picking the right berry or habitat seems obvious, as does the need for a preference derived from learning or innate aesthetic choice. Picking the right mate is at least as important. The identifying of best mate is driven by aesthetic tastes, as is identifying proper food and suitable habitat. Divergence is an important mechanism that reduces competition. I here posit that it would also be highly critical between sibling species that resemble each other, and would have implication in speciation. Tastes for mates have diverged widely, and routinely, because those who misidentified have left fewer genes in the gene pool. There is nothing arbitrary.

The *apparent* arbitrariness of the mating signal disappears in the ecological context, the area where previously isolated species reconnect. Differences then become adaptive. As in the evolution of habitat preference, by which divergence reduces competition, sexual-signal diversion implies selection for occupying different-signaling niches. Divergence is the clue to what aesthetics are, and why they are adaptive. Consider two well-known, closely related equids, the donkey and the horse. A female horse can mate with a male donkey, but their offspring, a mule, is sterile. In adaptive-evolutionary terms, it behooves (pun not intended) a female horse to not squander a mating possibility with a close species, when her potential offspring of it will never pass on *her* genes. Cross-matings would be especially devastating to monogamous or short-lived species, such as birds, which may live to breed only once or a few times in their life.

To be a successful breeder in a species of variable appearance — which naturally arises in separated populations — an animal must be able to detect a species-defining marker out of the mix of many potential signals. As a young amateur ornithologist, examining bird specimens in Berlin's Museum of Naturkunde that my father had collected in the 1930s in Celebes (now Sulawesi), I saw clear differences in at least one species of thrush, *Heinrichia calligyna*, that had been described by Erwin Stresemann, an eminent ornithologist at the time. Birds from one mountain versus another showed distinct differences of both size and color, but I could not say if they were the same or different species. Even trained taxonomists have trouble doing that, and Stresemann had apparently not differentiated them as distinct species, but I do not know how or why. However, I posit that the birds would have, and that their mate choices based on their aesthetic acumen were passed on to their offspring, who continued to evolve aesthetic tastes in mate choice based not on what the similar species have in common, but rather on how they differed and therefore how they would continue to differ even more in the future.*

Consider bumblebees as pseudo-sexual organs of plants. A species blooming at the same time and place as other plant species can induce pollinators to be flower-faithful only by differentiating its flower signals from those of its neighbors. Suppose competing plants had a simple platform flower that is colored red. If the bees saw the flowers of the two plant species as the same, the plants would be "mated" indiscriminately. The more that flowers of two adjacent species differ from each other, the greater probability that bees will be flower-faithful, and thus make more plant visits and raise the chances that seed will be fertilized, and offspring produced. Yes, the signal as such is totally arbitrary, but only if there is no competition, which is hardly ever the case.

The reproductive biology of plants has close parallels to that of birds, insects, and other animals, and the contrasts illuminate our understanding of their biology. Flowers that serve as aesthetic attention-getting ornaments evolved from leaves. All around the deep woods by my cabin in Maine, for example, some of the petals of bunchberry (*Cornus canadensis*) and hobblebush (*Viburnum lantanoides*) start out pale green as pseudo-leaves before they

---

* The idea came to me thirty years ago in Maine, during my field studies of the foraging behavior of bumblebees.

expand to become white and attention-getting. They are arranged in inflorescences where outer flowers are for show, lacking ovaries. Whether as individuals or as inflorescences, flower forms that serve as aesthetic attractants also have signposts and alleys and guardrails that physically guide pollinators to their reproductive organs; aesthetic and utilitarian functions merge.

With two very similar bird species living in close proximity, the same selection principles apply. The key issues are signaling to draw attention, maintaining fidelity to that signal, and having that signal stand out by a difference to enhance or promote fidelity — preferably, a huge difference — from the competing signals. In birds, courting features can be both visual and acoustic; in rodents, dogs, and insects they can be scent. Aesthetic symbols of beauty will in time diverge by natural selection based on fitness. If the aesthetics don't work, as apparently in many insects (and among some ducks and primates), there are differences in genitalia morphology that prohibit or discourage mating among different species, even if they try.

Animal-pollinated plants have numerous ovaries, with each adorned with specific allurements. These attracting ornaments usually shrivel and drop off within days or hours after fertilization. Retaining aesthetic ornaments on already-fertilized ovaries dilutes visitation to those not yet fertilized. That is, they have a cost if they are retained. Similarly, bird sexual allurements have the cost of attracting predators. But unlike plants, birds cannot afford to shed their sexual ornaments on short notice because feathers take a long time to produce, are costly, and have several other functions. However, birds can reserve their conspicuous showing off of their aesthetic ornaments for *specific* occasions or time periods.

Humans are perhaps the best demonstration of the ability to make rapid changes in aesthetics, and with the same object of mate choice. We have basic signals for sexual preferences (for example, body shapes) that may have been derived — as in the green leaves to flowers scenario — directly from utilitarian individual fitness. But like flowers' shapes, colors are now arbitrary and confer no survival benefits.

Particular songs or dances, with their physical enhancements evolved for fitness, derived from discriminating aesthetic senses of beauty. But an important point to note is that change happens. Fitness may be no more than the ability "to be glib at sixteen," as one of my professors once quipped. But consider the changing of styles, from time to time and from culture to culture: body types, grooming styles, cosmetics, fragrances, body adornment, body art, clothing. Perhaps similarly, male humpback whales advertise themselves by their unearthly and haunting songs. All those within hearing range sing the same complex song, but these songs change over the years, and all the whales adopt the new song. This pattern suggests an inherent love of novelty, or neophilia, an aesthetic for the new, which young ravens display and which is an adaptation for finding new food. As a result of this aesthetic, they can and do live in the widest habitat range of any animal, matching our own.

In sexual selection the aesthetic is necessarily conservative and highly specific. What attracts is what conforms and then defines a norm. However, it may change eventually, because when *all* are exactly alike, the unique or innovative starts to stand out, and that which *adds a little something draws attention*. It is what is looked at, heard, and noticed from out of the lineup. And once it is chosen, it is passed on (culturally, in the case of humans and whales). It becomes adaptive and may continue to evolve. However, although humans are of the primate order, I suspect our displays won't evolve to include bright red-and-blue faces like those of male Mandrill baboons (*Mandrillus sphinx*) or the robin's-egg-blue genitalia of male vervet monkeys (*Chlorocebus aethiops*). We are not unique, but we have our own, often seemingly erratic, aesthetic choices concerning food, habitat, mate, and art.

Seeing the Light in the Forest

Field Notes, a publication of the Field Naturalist and
Ecological Planning graduate program at the University of
Vermont, 2017

FEBRUARY 2017. AT DAWN A CHICKADEE SINGS, A DOWNY
woodpecker drums, and a red eastern horizon turns yellow. The
Beatles put it this way: "Here comes the sun" . . . "It's been a long
cold lonely winter . . ."

During the past months there has been little light. Scarcity can
be a good thing, because it can draw attention to what we may take
for granted. Scarcity forces us to fixate on what we miss. Right now
I really notice, and appreciate, the light. Most mornings throughout the winter I have gotten up in the dark, anxiously awaiting the
glow on the horizon. In the meantime, I've had to make do with
a faint flickering of rays from the woodstove onto the cabin floor.

Light is a band of the electromagnetic spectrum, and only part
of it is visible to us. We can't see the ultraviolet, nor the wood
stove's heat. But they are still there in real time. The light from
the stove comes from sunlight stored the year before. The light

I used while reading last evening had been captured the previous day, by the seven-by-seven-centimeter photovoltaic wafer on
a twenty-dollar inflatable Luci light, a marvel of technology that
catches and releases light by the push of a little button. This lamp's
light supply, captured the previous afternoon, first traveled eight
minutes and twenty seconds through space from the sun, where it
was produced by the collision of hydrogen atoms to create helium
by nuclear fusion.

The marvel of what a Luci light does is performed routinely by
the trees all around me. They store the energy of sunlight in molecular bonds in their wood, and hold it until they die and decay,
or until I release it through combustion in our stove. But this light
is captured by the chlorophyll molecule, a bio-light-catcher, in a
reaction that grabs carbon dioxide molecules out of the air while
also releasing oxygen. Photosynthesis stores the energy of the sun's
atomic fusion in the molecular fusion of the tree's wood.

Wood is an adaptation of the most amazing plants on earth, a
scaffolding that hoists solar-catching leaves high into the air. Each
tree races for sunlight against others doing the same thing. The
piece of maple burning in the stove next to me came from a tree
I culled over a year ago, enabling many others near it to grow. It
was made from light and carbon dioxide captured decades earlier.

Stored sunlight in the form of wood makes life possible here
in our off-the-grid cabin in the winter. Meanwhile, tanker trucks
drive daily up and down the road nearby, delivering cargoes of
hydrocarbons — from stored sunlight energy that was captured by
chlorophyll long before maple trees existed. We now mine that
light and energy from the ground, and are suddenly, and apparently irretrievably, committed to putting back into the atmosphere
what took hundreds of millions of years to sequester underground.

The oldest fossils on earth are those of photosynthetic organisms. The magic process made possible by chlorophyll put oxygen into our atmosphere and enabled the evolution of aerobic life. Oxygen now still comes to us mainly via plants, and forest plants are the major atmospheric keepers. Forests also create soil, and

Mixed species make a forest. Here, an oak and a white birch.

by way of their root networks, they capture and store water that would otherwise not stay on the land. They create atmosphere, climate, and habitat, the home and food for millions of species. It is no wonder that we may reflexively balk at the idea of cutting trees up to burn them, and perhaps we should. However, at the same time, considering the rest of the forest is just as crucial.

Trees are the most visible, but they are only one component of a forest. Obviously, we need more trees, and clear-cutting and plantations of vast tracts of land are poor substitutes for the ecological complexity of forests. But leaving them all untouched isn't the answer either.

We keep and grow forests because they have a direct and clearly perceived value. I'm passionate about trees, and not only because they are light incarnate. I also like paper, pears, apples and oranges, hazelnuts, timber frames, and wooden boats. I care about forests too, for their trees and for all that lives in, on, and around them. Growing a forest means harvesting trees by leaving trees, including the biggest of the best and the rare as well as the common, and allowing them to stay in place for their entire life spans.

The problem is not that we exploit trees. The problem is not use, but misuse, by destroying forests and replacing them with trees only. But if misuse were a reason to categorically abstain by credo, then one might as well prohibit having animals as companions, or having children. There is necessarily a cost to everything. It is the balance that counts, not just the ballast. Maybe that's seeing the light.

Index

Asian chestnut, 19
Asian honeybees, 89
Asian ladybird beetles, 73
athletes, 219–24
Audubon, John James, 11, 151
The Auk (bird journal), 144
auklets, 259
Australopithecus, 214

baboons, 274
balsam fir, 38
Bannister, Roger, 219
barn swallows, 263
bats, 118
Beamon, Bob, 219
bears, 75–76, 128, 200
The Beatles, 275
beauty, 267–74
bee-eaters, 213
bee-lining, 90–98
beech trees, 16, 17, 21, 30, 33
beechnut seeds, 12
bees. *See also* bumblebees; honeybees
    deceived by orchids, 103
    interdependence with flowers,
        236–37
    number of species, 77, 103
    pollination by, 28, 99–101, 103,
        240, 244, 271
beetles
    feeding on carrion, 108–11, 113–14
    fireflies, 233
    flight mechanism, 114–15
    ground beetles, 4–6, *5*
    ladybird beetles, 73, 121
    mating, 108–10
    moving carrion, 111–14, *113*
    scarab beetles, 104, 105–6, 115
    sudden movement, 243
    whirligig beetles, 116–22
    winter survival, 72
Beloperone californica, 58
Berkoff, David, 223
Beston, Henry, 9, 145
Betula alleghaniensis, 10–11

biological thermodynamics, 59–60,
    191, 196
birch trees, 277
    ice damage, 33–34, 37
    sap-lick, *162*
    seed production, 29
    yellow birch, 10–17
    "Birches" (Frost), 37
birds. *See also specific birds*
    brood parasitism, 154, 260–66
    caterpillar hunting, 52, 52n
    colors and displays, 231–32, 267,
        268–69, 272
    egg colors, 255–66
    leks, 232
    migration, 224
    synchronicity, 227–29, 231–32
Bishop, K. David, 182
black bindweed, 251–52
black-headed gulls, 257
blackbirds, 263
blackish nightjar, 181
Blem, Charles R., 171, 173
blood iris, 247
blowflies, 107, *113. See also* maggots
blue flag iris, 240, 241, 247
blue jays, 22–23, 28, 52, 52n
Bombus affinis, 83–84
Bombus hyperboreus, 78
Bombus polaris, 77, 78, 79, 81, 82
Bombus terricola, 84
Boston, Ralph, 219
bottle flies, 107, *113*
bramblings, 260
Brewer, Lawrence, 20
broad-winged hawk, *165*
brood parasitism, 154, 260–66
brown-headed cowbirds, 154, 261–64
Bubo (owl), 69, *70*
bullfrogs, 230
bumblebees
    Alaska, 82–83
    brood care, 80–81
    Canadian Arctic, 75–82
    coevolution, 100–101